PIE

Dean Brettschneider is a professional baker, pâtissier and entrepreneur. Arguably one of the world's best bakers, Dean is truly a global baker. He was based in Shanghai for several years and now resides in Denmark and New Zealand, where he heads up his global baking empire, and travels regularly to the United Kingdom where he is a consultant. Dean is also the founder and co-owner of the global bakery chain Baker & Cook, which has its flagship store in Singapore (www.bakerandcook.biz). Dean is the author of several award-winning books on baking, and is involved in a number of television programmes that promote baking excellence.

www.globalbaker.com

PIE

DELICIOUS SWEET AND SAVOURY PIES AND PASTRIES,
FROM STEAK AND ONION PIE TO PECAN TART

Global Baker
Dean Brettschneider

Photography by Aaron McLean

jacqui
small

First published in the UK in 2013 by:
Jacqui Small LLP
An imprint of Aurum Press
74–77 White Lion Street
London N1 9PF

First published by Penguin Group (NZ), 2012

Designed and typeset by Anna Egan-Reid, © Penguin Group (NZ)
Prepress by Image Centre Ltd

ISBN 978 1 909342 18 7

A catalogue record for this book is available from the British Library.

2015 2014 2013
10 9 8 7 6 5 4 3 2 1

Printed in China by 1010 Printing

Contents

Introduction

I grew up with pies for lunch from the high school tuck shop. I remember that lukewarm, runny minced beef and gravy-like filling encased in a soggy, under-baked, doughy pastry wrapped in a cellophane-sealed bag that was kept in a pie warmer (or heated from frozen in a pie warmer set at 60°C, which is the holding temperature, not the heating temperature!). Sometimes it was still frozen in the middle and usually squashed. Thank goodness for tomato sauce, which we squirted all over it to make it edible!

Another childhood memory is of Mum buying a family pie from the supermarket. What a treat it was, unbaked in a large aluminium foil tray the size of a dinner plate. If I remember correctly, it was called a Mince Family Plate Pie. We would heat the oven up, brush the pie with milk (there was no mention of egg wash) to get a glaze, shove it in the oven, bake it until it looked brown and then serve it with mashed potatoes and boiled minted peas.

Then along came the microwave pie . . . funnily enough, in my early days of product development for an industrial pie maker, I was involved in the science behind making pastry crispy in the microwave.

Let's just say thank goodness times have moved on to a point where quality really does matter.

There is nothing more satisfying than eating a piping hot, freshly baked pie, tart, quiche or even sausage roll, out of the kitchen oven, brimming with various fillings enclosed in a buttery pastry. Or one left to cool down slightly and eaten warm, or allowed to fully cool before being decorated with pastry cream, fresh cream, fruits, nuts, dusted with icing sugar or even glazed with an apricot glaze to take it from ordinary to extraordinary.

Pies in many shapes and sizes are made around the globe and are the most-baked product in the home kitchen – the world is full of home bakers making their favourite pies for themselves, families and friends.

Traditional pies, which have been handed down in grandmothers' old recipe books, are popular again. Then there are the new versions with modern twists on the classics, using newly available ingredients and flavour combinations to wake up the taste buds. Pies are even now becoming part of the menu in fine-dining restaurants. The humble pie is coming back with passion.

The pies, tarts, pastries and the 'not-quite-a-pie' pies in this book are mostly based on traditional recipes but have been given that familiar twist, either to the filling combinations or the pastry, that I am known for in my global, new world baking style.

How to use this book

In the following chapters, and in the Basic Recipes at the back of the book, I take time to unlock quite a few basics on the making and baking of pastry. I can't stress enough that, in order for you to succeed, you need to take the time to read all about the ingredients, the equipment and, most importantly, the basic processes and techniques necessary to make pastries and pies. I would even go so far as to suggest that you keep the book beside your bed for your night-time reading.

Sweet, short and puff pastry are all used in this book – some basic and some innovative, with many flavour twists and combinations. Once the basics are mastered, don't be scared to mix and match the pastries to suit yourself – nothing is set in stone.

When making any of the pastries, I recommend you double or triple the recipe and divide it into smaller batches. Wrap each portion of pastry in clingfilm and place in the freezer until needed, then just remove from the freezer, thaw and use as described in the recipe. Pastry freezes exceptionally well, so make life easy and think ahead.

And as for the question everyone wants to ask me . . . can you use store-bought pastry? The answer is yes, of course, it's your choice – but also it's all part of the experience to make your own!

Happy pie making and baking.
Global Baker – Dean Brettschneider
www.globalbaker.com

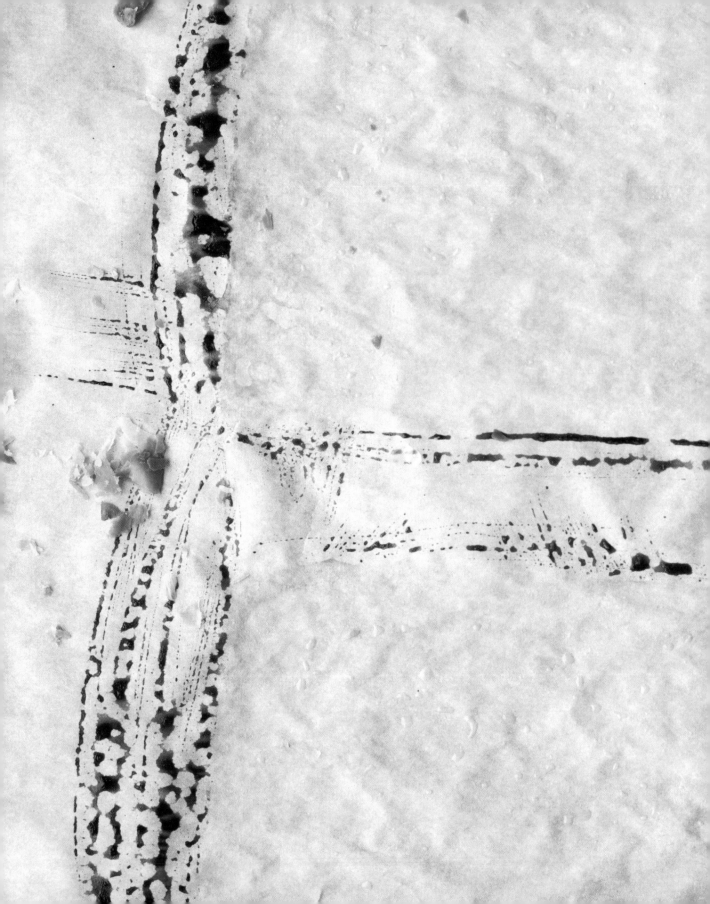

The History of the Humble Pie

The Pie in History

Firstly the question should be asked: what is a pie? The Oxford Dictionary describes it as: 'A baked food consisting of one or two layers or crusts of pastry with a filling'.

It's interesting to note that the first recorded use of the word 'pie' relating to food was as far back as 1303, and by 1362 the pie was well known and popular as a food medium. But when was the first 'pie' reputed to have been made? Let's take a brief journey back in time.

The pie can be traced back in history to the ancient Egyptians. They were prepared and baked by the Pharaohs' bakers, who encased fillings in bread dough, which was considered a primitive form of pastry dough. These early pies consisted of fillings based on field plants and grains and, if sweetening was required, honey was the key, sought-after ingredient. Even the pie then was considered a delicacy.

It's widely understood that the Greeks were the first makers of 'pie pastry' as such. It was prepared by forming flour and water into a very simple dough, which was in turn wrapped around well-seasoned meats. This pastry encasement served to retain the baking juices within and around the meat fillings. However, this pastry casing was not always intended to be eaten; it served to contain the filling and its varying flavour releases during the baking process.

It is believed that by 100 BC the pie had arrived in Rome. One of the earliest fillings noted by historians was goat's cheese and honey. Until this period pies had been fully encased by one outer dough piece, and it is thought that the Romans were the first to make pies with a top and bottom layer around the fillings. However, while both forms of encasement allowed for the preparation of very good fillings, due to the properties of the encased chamber concept, the pastry tended to be discarded rather than eaten.

While not having an exact date to go by, in medieval northern Europe a pastry recipe was later developed using fat in the form of lard and/or butter. This improved the eating and handling properties of the pastry. Lard, in particular, gave the pie dough some resilience and shape retention when not baked in a baking pan or high-sided dish. While there is still some uncertainty around this, it is believed actual pastry recipes became available from the middle of the sixteenth century. Some research, however, finds that the first recipe may not have become available until 1596.

Not surprisingly, therefore, in what was and is a very passionate and creative environment and a proud profession, a number of countries lay claim to the creation of the first pie. On record is a Frenchman, Antonin Carême, who during the period of 1784–1833, elevated French pastry-making to an iconic art form that endures today. For example, nowadays one of the recipes for puff pastry production is called 'The French Method'.

The meat pie has been part of English cuisine since medieval times. Pie fillings in twelfth-century Britain consisted of beef or mutton; these were followed by game birds and domestic poultry. It is documented that in London in 1850 the first 'eel and pie' shop was opened. The English claim ownership of the introduction of the steak and kidney filling combination, and the Cornish pasty

is also a first belonging to Britain. While not a pie by definition, it is a filling encased in a pastry dough of sorts and is baked free-standing as were the very early pies. (It's interesting to note that most early research indicates that pies were baked, not cooked: raw fillings, as opposed to precooked fillings, were positioned within the dough and then sealed to cook within the baked casing.)

Small pies are often referred to as tartlets but, back in medieval times, a tartlet was a shallow but large open pie. Another common term for a pie was a 'coffin' because of the shape of the lidded baking container. 'Traps' were pies with no tops. Ancient Egyptian pies were commonly called 'galettes'. The one relatively common theme drawn from all these names is that over generations of pie-baking the shape of the pie has changed very little.

Many early pies had a national or iconic ingredient present in the recipe. For example, the 'Irish Pie' is commonly referred to as the 'steak and Guinness pie', in which part of the filling consists

of Guinness, bacon and onions. The pumpkin pie, one of America's iconic pies, was created in 1623. Another American classic is, of course, the apple pie.

A pie is not just about the filling preparation but the methodology employed to brown the pastry – and this is not always achieved by baking it in an oven. An example of this is seen in Latin America, where pies have their own traditional fillings, but can be either baked or fried.

Today mention is often made of the 'gourmet pie', but when you look at early notes on the preparation of pie fillings, it is clear that the gourmet pie has always been with us in one form or other in that cooks, bakers and pâtisserie chefs have and continue to strive for the ultimate flavour blends. While the art of the encasement may have been refined, and there are many definitions of what constitutes a pastry (rustic or otherwise), a pie is still all about the flavour and the eating properties. One can imagine the Pharaohs were a lot less forgiving about any non-conformance with this.

Paul Hansen

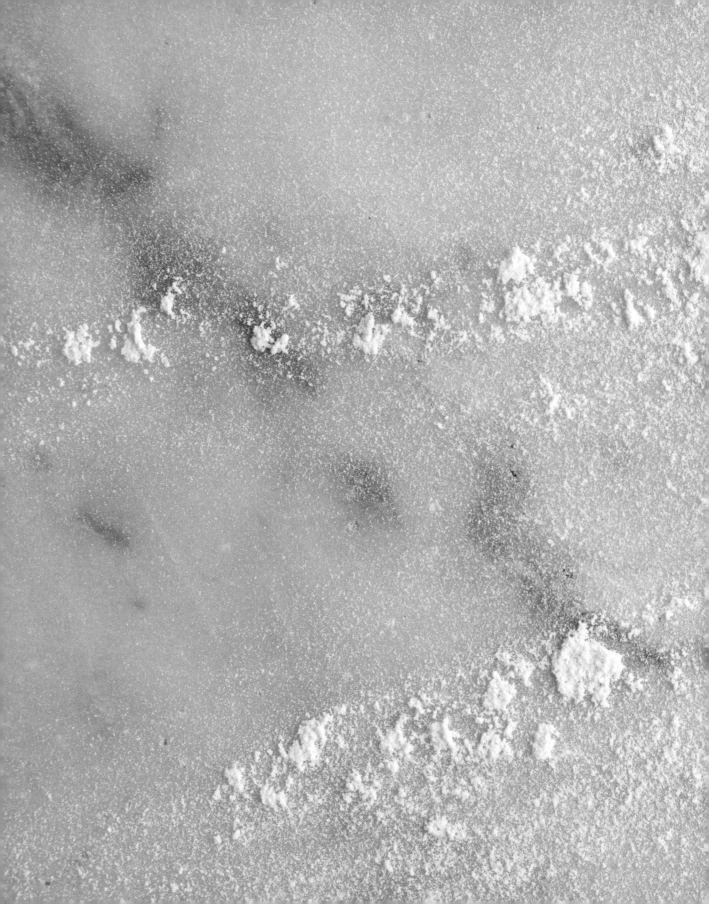

Ingredients

Basic Ingredients

Puff Pastry

There are four basic ingredients used in the manufacture of puff pastry:

- strong flour
- butter
- salt
- water.

Often the only other ingredients used are lemon juice or cream of tartar.

Short and Sweet Pastry

Short and sweet pastries are made using a completely different manufacturing procedure and this is reflected in the ingredients used:

- standard plain flour
- butter or margarine
- salt
- sugar (for sweet pastry)
- egg and/or water.

Other ingredients can include baking powder, cocoa for chocolate sweet pastry and lemon zest or vanilla extract for flavour.

Basic Ingredient Functions

Flour is important because its protein-forming potential dictates the lift that will be obtained, and because it forms the final structure of the pastry. For both puff and choux pastry, strong flour should be used for its strength and good-quality protein (gluten). In the case of short and sweet pastry, a medium or strong flour is suitable. Its high percentage of fat or butter softens and weakens the protein (gluten), allowing the pastry to become more biscuit-like.

Salt improves the flavour and has a strengthening effect upon the protein (gluten), which is required for puff and choux pastry.

Butter has different functions in different pastries.

Puff Pastry: Butter is used in the dough stage to make the dough softer and easier to handle. It also makes the finished pastry more tender and shorter to eat. Butter is used to separate the layers of dough and influence the lift of the pastry and also have an effect on the eating quality of the baked pastry. This butter is often referred to as the layering fat. The amount of layering fat varies from 50–100 per cent based on the flour weight.

In commercial terms, we usually define the type of pastry made by the amount of layering fat used:

- Half puff pastry: 50 per cent of layering fat based on flour weight.
- Three-quarter puff pastry: 75 per cent of layering fat based on flour weight.
- Full puff pastry: 100 per cent of layering fat based on flour weight.

Short and Sweet Pastry: Butter is used to shorten and weaken the protein (gluten), allowing the pastry to be more biscuit-like in texture, similar to shortbread.

Water is largely required to obtain the correct consistency of the dough. Water also hydrates the protein (gluten) and allows it to become elastic and extensible. The amount used depends upon the absorption rate of the flour, the amount of fat used in the dough and the process used.

Sugar is mainly used in the manufacture of sweet pastry, which requires a sweeter tasting finished product. Sugar in conjunction with butter has a softening and shortening effect on the protein (gluten). The higher the sugar percentage, the crispier and more biscuit-like the sweet pastry will be. Caster sugar is always used to ensure the sugar crystals dissolve.

Eggs are generally not used in the manufacture of puff pastry, but are essential in sweet pastry. In sweet pastry, eggs are mainly used to enrich the dough for quality. Eggs also improve the handling qualities of sweet pastry when thinly rolling and pressing it into tart moulds, etc.

Baking powder adds lightness and apparent shortness to sweet pastry. In top-quality sweet pastry this is not necessary.

Cream of tartar and lemon juice are both acids which have a toughening but mellowing effect on the protein (gluten), allowing extensibility when rolling out the pastry, resulting in improved volume. If using either one of these acids, ensure you do not use an excessive amount, as this will turn your puff pastry sour and result in a low volume. If using good quality flour, the addition of acid is not required.

Spices may be added to all pastries, mainly to contribute to the taste and flavour and also to change the colour. If used in excess, they can leave an undesirable taste when eating.

Herbs, both dried and fresh, can be added to all styles of pastry and the choice is only dependent on whether they are sweet or savoury influenced. Experimenting is the key, as there are no general rules for how much to add other than personal preference.

Nuts can be added to pastry. Almonds and hazelnuts are the most commonly used nuts, especially in sweet and short pastry. When nuts are added to the flour component they are ground first into a powder (sometimes called a meal). If left whole, nuts will cause holes in the pastry. Sliced nuts or nibs are often used post-baking or as decoration. Nuts also form many fillings that are used in tarts, such as frangipane (or almond cream).

Grains and seeds are a great way to get some health into your indulgence. They also have a feel-good factor. When adding grains, you may need to allow for additional water as many grains are dried and tend to take up the water in the dough, which is actually needed to make the dough easy to

work with. Therefore it is advisable to soak dried grains in half their weight of water for at least two hours before adding them to the other ingredients. Seeds, on the other hand, don't require pre-soaking. Both grains and seeds are used for flavour and in particular provide a rustic, earthy nuttiness to the pastry. They can also be used as toppings before and after baking.

Equipment

Your Hands

These are the two most important pieces of equipment that you have in your 'tool box'. Your hands must be strong and firm, yet gentle and sensitive; able to feel when the dough is fully mixed, elastic and at the same time smooth and silky to the touch; as well as being light and delicate enough to gently fold and lift the softest of flours through a perfectly aerated batter.

You need to have a good feeling for temperature and consistency when using your hands. By making the same recipe more than once, you will develop the 'baker's feel' and know when it feels right to stop folding the flour into your delicate, light-as-air sponge or when to put the loaf of bread in the oven, not to mention being able to tell if your product is under-baked, perfectly baked or over-baked.

I often see people working with scrapers, mixers, spoons and knives, too scared to touch the dough or batter because they will get messy and dirty. Go on, get right in there, and don't underestimate the value of using your hands in baking!

Scales

As with all recipes, the more accurately you measure the more chance you have of gaining perfect results. A good set of digital scales is one of the best pieces of cooking and baking equipment you can have. Treat them well and you will have them for many, many years. I recommend digital scales with one-gram increments.

Sieves

When combining dry ingredients it's best to sift them together in a large mixing bowl to ensure even distribution. This is particularly important when using raising agents, such as baking powder and bicarbonate of soda, and spices and cocoa powders. Always have on hand a small fine sieve that you can use to dust icing sugar on top of baked pies and tarts for decorating.

Mixing Bowls

There is nothing more frustrating than trying to mix your ingredients in a mixing bowl that is too small. Always have on hand a range of mixing bowls from very large to small.

Pie-baking Tins, Tartlet Moulds and Flan Cases

Have on hand a range of pie dishes at different sizes and heights, from individual pies to large family ones to suit every occasion. You can get a great range of both domestic and professional pie tins, tart moulds and flan cases today in speciality kitchen stores. Don't discount mini and standard muffin tins as they make great individual pies – and a 20cm round high-sided cake tin is perfect for that deep-dish pie. Do try to purchase Teflon-lined tins as these really make life easy, but take care not to scratch the surface when washing them.

Baking Trays

Always use a strong heavy tray that actually holds its heat and is solid. Sometimes, when wanting extra heat on the base of your pie, you should place a baking tray in the oven for at least 30 minutes before putting the pie tin on top of it. The solid heat will help to bake the base of your pie.

Silicone Mats and Non-stick Baking Paper

Non-stick baking mats (which are mostly silicone mats) are important if you are baking free-form tarts. Alternatively, you can use non-stick baking paper. Take care not to cut on your non-stick baking mat as this will ruin it. They are expensive but should last a lifetime.

Non-stick baking paper is also good when baking blind. You can use it again and again before discarding it.

If the top of your pie or tart is becoming too dark and the bottom remains unbaked, place a sheet of non-stick baking paper on top to prevent it burning.

Baking Beans

When baking blind (see page 214) you need baking beans to weigh down the pastry. This prevents it rising upwards and the sides shrinking downwards. You can purchase specialised ceramic baking beans, but rice or dried beans also work perfectly well and can be used over and over again.

Knives, Scrapers, Whisks, Cutters and Spoons

You will need to assemble a combination of your favourite knives, scrapers, cutters, teaspoons, measuring cups, wooden spoons and whisks. This is very much a personal choice, as during your years of baking, you will no doubt collect many different pieces of small equipment.

Electric Mixer

Do you need a great big expensive mixer? If you can afford one, then yes, but if not, the pastries and pies in this book can be made by hand. The only time it is essential to use an electric mixer is when you mix a sponge or make an icing that needs to be light, fluffy and airy, thus the need for using the whisk and beater attachment.

Pastry Brushes

A pastry brush is mainly used for applying egg wash before baking or applying an apricot glaze after baking for that golden shine. Also, don't forget it's the best way to apply water to pastry to stick it together. When decorating, brushing on water acts like a glue for things to stick to.

Measuring Jugs, Cups and Spoons

Jugs are great for measuring liquids. Water and milk measure the same in weight (grams) as they do in volume (millilitres). It's also easier to pour liquid fillings into a pastry-lined tin from a jug than a bowl.

Measuring spoons are handy for those small dry measurements that your digital scales might not pick up.

Ruler

Always keep a good strong ruler in your baking equipment drawer to use when you need to find a certain size of tin or cut out your pastry to a particular size.

Pastry Wheels

Pastry wheels come with a straight or crinkled edge: both are great when cutting out lines of pastry for a trellis top. Or you can get specialist pastry trellis cutters for sweet and puff pastry from specialist cookware shops.

Cookie Cutters

A good set of plain and scalloped cookie cutters is great for both decorating and cutting pastry to fit your small individual tartlet moulds or tins.

Cooling Rack

A must in all pie-baking. Once your pie has cooled in the dish, it should be removed and placed on a cooling rack to completely cool. If you leave it in the pie dish for too long, the pastry can sweat and the bottom will become soggy and often stick to the dish. However, if you will need to re-warm your pie, it's often best to leave it in the dish until reheating is required.

Oven Thermometer

Always have a good oven thermometer to place in different parts of the oven so you can tell what is happening and what temperature the oven really is.

Oven

There is no need for the home baker to invest thousands of dollars in a 'state of the art' oven – you can easily make a few adjustments to your existing oven. (For example, to create steam in your oven, you can either spray the oven walls with warm water from a spray bottle or simply throw some ice cubes in a preheated baking tin at the bottom of the oven. This creates a steamy, humid environment for your bread to bake in. Of course, you do not need to do this for pastries, tarts, biscuits or cakes.)

Before placing anything in the oven, always check that it is set at the correct temperature for your baking and that it is up to that temperature.

Note: All recipes in this book are based on a standard oven (without a fan). If using a fan-assisted oven, then reduce the temperature by 10–15°C and take care as the baking time will also be reduced.

Meat Pies

Mince and Cheese Pies

Use a strong, full, mature Cheddar for a bold cheese flavour for these pies. The commercial shop-bought pies often have a runny pumpable cheese sauce – I can only imagine what's in it to make it like that!

MAKES 4 INDIVIDUAL LUNCH-SIZE PIES

PASTRY

1 quantity of Butter Puff Pastry (see page 203)

FILLING

1 tbsp olive oil

1 tbsp butter

1 medium onion, finely chopped

2 cloves garlic, peeled and crushed

500g lean beef mince

30g standard plain flour

175ml beef stock, ready-made is fine

125ml lager

2 tbsp tomato purée

1 tbsp Marmite (optional)

1 tsp balsamic vinegar

¼ tsp dried mixed herbs

salt and pepper, to taste

200g tasty cheese or Cheddar, grated

1 egg beaten with 2 tbsp water, for egg wash

2 tbsp black or white sesame seeds for the topping

Make Butter Puff Pastry the day before and store wrapped in the refrigerator. Cut off a quarter of the pastry block and set it aside for the pie lids. On a lightly floured surface, roll out the larger piece of pastry to a square, approximately 4mm thick. Cut the square into quarters. Line each individual pie dish, ensuring the pastry is firmly pressed against the sides and leaving some hanging over the edge of the dishes. Roll out the smaller piece of pastry to a square, approximately 3mm thick. Cut the square into quarters, cover with clingfilm and set aside.

Heat the oil and butter in a large frying pan, then add the onion and garlic and cook until the onion is golden. Add the beef mince and cook until well browned, stirring occasionally to prevent large lumps of meat forming. Stir in the flour and cook for approximately 30 seconds. Gradually add the beef stock and beer, then bring to the boil. Add the tomato purée or paste and Marmite (if using), balsamic vinegar, mixed herbs, and salt and pepper to taste. Lower the heat and simmer gently for 10 minutes, then remove from the heat and allow to cool.

Fill each pastry-lined dish almost up to the top with the mince filling, then add a small handful of grated tasty cheese or Cheddar.

Brush the edge of the pastry bases with water and place the lids on top. Seal edges and trim off any excess pastry with a sharp knife. Brush the tops of the pastry with egg wash and sprinkle with sesame seeds. Rest for 1–2 hours (or longer) before baking.

Bake in a preheated 220°C (gas mark 7) oven for 25–30 minutes or until pastry is crisp and golden-brown in colour. Allow to cool in the dishes for 10 minutes, then remove from dishes and place on a cooling rack.

Serve with your favourite tomato sauce and a crisp green salad or bowl of French fries.

Spanish Chicken Pie

**The suet in this pie adds a touch of old world pastry-making technique.
It made the most tender, delicate pastry when combined with self-raising flour.
I like to serve this pie with rice and buttered spinach or
a potato salad with cold French beans tossed in vinaigrette.**

MAKES A LARGE PIE, SERVING 6 PEOPLE

PASTRY

100g prepared suet (available in the supermarket and normally blended with flour) or margarine

200g self-raising flour

4 tbsp white wine

large pinch of salt

FILLING

8 chicken thighs on the bone

salt and freshly ground pepper

2 tbsp olive oil

knob of butter

2 small red onions, chopped

2 stalks celery, chopped

2 red peppers, cored, deseeded and sliced

1 fennel bulb, sliced

8 cloves garlic, chopped

good pinch of saffron

2 tsp paprika

1 large glass red wine, about 300ml

1 × 400g tin plum tomatoes

GLAZE

1 egg, beaten, for egg wash

Make the pastry by mixing the suet or margarine, flour, white wine and salt together in a large bowl until a soft dough forms. Add a little more flour if the dough is sticky, or wine if it is too dry. Knead the dough for a couple of minutes until it becomes smooth and a little elastic. Cover with clingfilm and allow to chill in the refrigerator.

Season the chicken with salt and pepper. Heat the oil in a large saucepan and fry the chicken pieces until they are slightly brown. Remove from the saucepan and set aside. Add the butter to the saucepan and stir in the onion, celery, red pepper and fennel. Leave them to stew gently for 15 minutes, stirring occasionally and checking that they do not burn or stick to the pan. Mix in the garlic, saffron and paprika. After 2 minutes, pour in the red wine and tomatoes. Season with a pinch of salt and a few grinds of black pepper.

Return the chicken to the saucepan and simmer for 30 minutes, stirring from time to time to make sure it does not stick. Allow the mixture to cool, then take the chicken pieces out of the sauce.

Pull the chicken meat from the bones with your fingers, discarding the skin and bones. Cut the meat into bite-sized pieces and stir it back into the sauce. Season the mixture to taste. Pour it into a pie dish and set aside to cool slightly.

Roll out the pastry so that it will cover the pie dish. Brush the rim of the dish with a little beaten egg and place the pastry over the pie. Trim the edges, putting aside any trimmings, and brush the top of the pastry with a little egg. Press the edges down using the tines of a fork.

Cut pastry shapes from the extra pastry and decorate the top of the pie. Cut a hole in the top to let steam escape and brush all over with the rest of the egg.

Bake in a preheated 220°C (gas mark 7) oven for 40 minutes. Check after 15 minutes. If the pastry is turning golden, cover with aluminium foil and continue baking.

Sausage, Sun-dried Tomato and Potato Tart

This is one of my favourites simply because it looks absolutely stunning, making me just want to grab a slice and eat it. It's as rustic as they come. Enjoy with a nice glass of crisp, fruity Sauvignon Blanc – it doesn't need anything else.

MAKES A 22CM TART, SERVING 4–6 PEOPLE

PASTRY
1 quantity of Basic Short Pastry (see page 197)

FILLING
3 tbsp olive oil

3 onions, thinly sliced

2 cloves garlic, finely chopped

3 tbsp water

200g waxy potatoes, peeled and chopped

350g best-quality fresh pork sausages

1 tbsp standard plain flour

2–3 tbsp tomato purée

12 sun-dried tomato halves in oil, chopped

1 tsp dried chilli flakes

2 tsp dried Herbes de Provence

sea salt and freshly ground black pepper, to taste

100g mascarpone

Make Basic Short Pastry and bring to room temperature, if necessary. Roll out the pastry on a lightly floured surface, then use it to line a 22cm round tart tin (4cm deep). Prick the base, then chill or freeze for 15 minutes. Line the tart with aluminium foil and place baking blind material inside. Bake blind (see page 214) in a preheated 200°C (gas mark 6) oven for 15–20 minutes or until the pastry is baked through. Remove the foil and weights and place the tin back in the oven for 5 minutes.

To make the filling, heat the oil in a large saucepan, then add the onion, garlic and water. Cover and cook over gentle heat for about 1 hour or until onion is meltingly soft but not coloured. Stir occasionally to prevent them from catching and burning. Remove from the heat and let cool.

Blanch the potatoes in boiling, salted water for 1 minute, then drain and set aside. Remove the skins from the sausages. Heat a non-stick frying pan and add the sausagemeat, breaking it up with a fork or wooden spoon as it cooks and browns.

After about 5 minutes, stir in the flour, tomato purée, sun-dried tomatoes, chilli, herbs, salt and pepper. Cook for a further 5 minutes, then stir in the potato. Spoon the mixture into the pastry case and dot with small spoonfuls of the mascarpone and cooked onion. Rough it up a little to give it a rustic look.

Bake in a preheated 220°C (gas mark 7) oven for 25–30 minutes or until golden in colour.

Steak, Caramelised Onion and Red Pepper Mustard Pies

I was first introduced to this pie in the early 2000s, when gourmet pies were becoming popular. It still sits among my favourite steak pies simply because of the tangy red pepper mustard sauce and the sweetness of the caramelised onion.

MAKES 4 INDIVIDUAL PIES

PASTRY
1 quantity of Butter Puff Pastry
(see page 203)

CARAMELISED ONION
1 large onion, peeled
15g butter
10g light soft brown sugar

FILLING
50g butter
70g standard plain flour
350ml milk
1½ tsp mustard powder
1 tsp freshly ground black pepper
½ tsp salt
400g beef topside
80g wholegrain mustard
2 small cloves garlic, crushed
120g chopped red pepper

GLAZE
1 egg beaten with 1 tbsp water,
for egg wash

Make Butter Puff Pastry ahead and rest it as required. Divide the pastry in half and roll one half out to 2–4mm thick on a lightly floured surface. Line four individual pie dishes with the pastry. On a lightly floured surface, roll out the other half of the pastry to 3mm thick and cut into four equal pieces for your tops. Lightly dust each disc with flour, put between clingfilm, cover and place in the refrigerator until required.

To caramelise the onion, slice the onion and set aside. Melt the butter in a frying pan over a medium heat and add the sugar. Add the onion to the butter and sugar mixture, and allow it to soften and turn a light golden colour, stirring occasionally. This should take approximately 20 minutes. Remove from the heat and cool. Set aside until later. This can be made a day in advance and kept in the refrigerator.

To make the filling, place the butter in a saucepan and melt over a medium heat. Add the flour to the butter, and blend until a firm ball of dough is formed and the saucepan is left clean. Slowly add a little of the milk and mix in thoroughly. Keep adding small quantities of milk, mixing in each addition thoroughly to prevent lumps. Once all the milk is added to make a runny sauce or roux, add the mustard powder, freshly ground black pepper and salt. Mix together and set aside until required.

Cut beef into cubes and cook in its own juices in a saucepan. Once the meat is cooked, add enough flour to soak up all the juices.

Heat the roux over a moderate heat, stirring constantly until it reaches a thick consistency. Add the wholegrain mustard, garlic and red pepper. Mix until all the ingredients are blended together.

Continues overleaf

Add some of the thick sauce to the meat, stir in and then mix the remainder of the sauce into the meat. Allow to cool or cover and place overnight in the refrigerator.

Place some beef filling mixture into each pie base and fill to three-quarters. Add a layer of caramelised onion, then brush the edge of each pastry base with egg wash and place the pastry lid on top. Seal edges and trim away any excess pastry with a sharp knife.

Cut slits in the top of each pie using a sharp knife to let steam escape and brush the top surface with egg wash. Rest for 1 hour (or longer) before baking.

Bake in a preheated 220°C (gas mark 7) oven for 30 minutes. Allow to cool in the pie dishes for 30 minutes, then remove and place on a cooling rack.

Classic Bacon and Egg Pie

Here I have taken an iconic home-baked pie that almost everyone has experienced at some point and given it a new look with the smoky, spicy orange paprika pastry. The black sesame seeds give extra bite and colour so that it's like an old car with a new paint job!

MAKES A 24CM ROUND DEEP PIE, SERVING 6–8 PEOPLE

PASTRY
1 quantity of Smoked Paprika and Black Sesame Seed Puff Pastry (see page 206)

FILLING
50g tasty cheese
10 slices farmhouse-style bacon
12–15 eggs
5 tbsp each very finely chopped fresh parsley and basil
salt and freshly ground black pepper, to taste
2 large firm but ripe tomatoes, thinly sliced

Make Smoked Paprika and Black Sesame Seed Puff Pastry the day before and store wrapped in the refrigerator.

Place a baking tray on the lower shelf of the oven and preheat it to 210°C (gas mark 6). The pie can be placed directly on the tray, which helps the pastry base to bake right the way through.

Divide the pastry in two, one piece slightly larger than the other. On a floured surface, roll out the larger piece and ease into a 24cm fluted deep pie dish or flan ring with a removable base.

Roll out the remaining pastry into a circle large enough to form the top, lightly flour and roll up in clingfilm. Set aside in the refrigerator.

Finely grate the cheese and scatter over the pastry-lined base. Remove the rind from the bacon and cut into strips. Place half the strips in an even layer over the cheese. Take all but one of the eggs and break them one at a time, placing directly on top of the bacon. Try not to break the yolks.

Scatter the herbs evenly over the eggs. Sprinkle liberally with salt and pepper, and layer over slices of tomato and the remaining strips of bacon.

Place the chilled pastry on top to form a top crust.

Break the remaining egg into a cup and beat it with a fork. Use a little of the beaten egg to seal the top pastry to the base by brushing the underside of the top pastry and gently pressing the top to the sides. Cut slits in the top of the pie using a sharp knife and brush the remaining beaten egg over the top to glaze the pie.

For best results, leave the prepared pie to rest for 1 hour before baking or, even better, overnight in the refrigerator.

Bake in the preheated oven for 45–50 minutes or until the pastry is crisp and golden-brown in colour. Allow to stand for at least 20 minutes before removing from the tin.

Untraditional Shepherd's Pies

**Think of this as having all the elements of a classic
Shepherd's Pie but just given my 'new world' baking twist in terms
of design and presentation. I love it and so will you.**

MAKES 4 × 500ML PRESERVING JARS

FILLING
1 tbsp olive oil
1 large onion, chopped
2 medium carrots, diced
2 tbsp flour
500g lean minced lamb or beef
2 tbsp tomato purée
1 tbsp fresh thyme leaves
1 generous splash Worcestershire sauce
500ml beef stock
salt and pepper, to taste

CRISPY HERB POTATOES
800g potatoes, scrubbed clean
2 tbsp olive oil
2 cloves garlic, finely chopped
1 tbsp chopped rosemary
1 tbsp thyme leaves
salt and pepper, to taste
4 tbsp chopped chives
100g tasty cheese, grated

Heat the oil in a medium saucepan, then add the onion and carrot and cook for a few minutes. Stir in the flour and cook for a few minutes while stirring. When the carrots are soft, turn up the heat, add the mince and brown, stirring to ensure all the mince is broken up in crumbly bits.

Add the tomato purée, thyme and Worcestershire sauce and fry for a few minutes. Pour over the stock and bring to a simmer. Reduce the heat to low, then cover and cook for 40 minutes, uncovering halfway and stirring occasionally throughout. Season with salt and pepper to taste. Keep hot, ready to use, while you are preparing the Crispy Herb Potatoes.

Wash and scrub the potatoes and cut into halves or quarters, then boil in plenty of salted water for 10–15 minutes until tender, but still a little firm (not too soft as you need to fry them). Drain and cool a little before cutting into small rough cubes.

In a heavy-based frying pan, heat the oil until hot, then add the garlic, potatoes, rosemary and thyme and fry until crisp and golden-brown in colour. Season with salt and pepper and toss with half of the chives.

Spoon the hot mince filling evenly into the preserving jars, top with a good sprinkle of grated cheese and the rest of the chives and then top with the Crispy Herb Potatoes. Lightly season again and serve immediately.

Chicken and Pork Pies with Rocket Pesto and Pear Mostarda

The magic of these pies lies in the fact that they are a complete twist on the traditional pork pie. Combining chicken with pork, the modern transformation is taken a step further by serving them with rocket pesto and a lovely pear mostarda.

MAKES 8 INDIVIDUAL PIES

PEAR MOSTARDA
150g caster sugar
1 tbsp brown mustard seeds
4 tsp Dijon mustard
2 bay leaves
pinch of cayenne pepper
1 tbsp vegetable oil
large pinch of salt
160ml cold water
2 firm but ripe pears, peeled, cored and diced into 1cm cubes
125g dried apricots, quartered

PASTRY
1 quantity of Hot Water Pastry (see page 200)

FILLING
800g skinless chicken breast, finely diced
500g minced pork
300g bacon, rind removed and finely chopped
1 onion, finely chopped
6 cloves garlic, finely chopped
40g flat-leaf parsley, finely chopped
20g sage leaves, finely chopped
1 tbsp finely chopped rosemary
zest of 2 lemons
salt and white pepper, to taste
8 tbsp rocket pesto

GLAZE
1 egg beaten with 1 tbsp water, for egg wash

Make the Pear Mostarda a day ahead. Combine the sugar, mustard seeds, 2 tsp mustard, bay leaves, cayenne pepper, oil, salt and water in a medium saucepan and bring to a simmer over medium-high heat. Reduce heat to medium. Add the fruit and cook, stirring occasionally, until the liquid has evaporated and the fruit is glossy (20–25 minutes). Stir in the remaining mustard, season to taste and refrigerate for at least 24 hours. Bring to room temperature to serve.

Make Hot Water Pastry ahead, roll into one large disc and rest it as required. Set aside one-quarter of the pastry and roll out the remainder to 4–5mm thick. Cut eight rectangles or round circles large enough to fit a rectangular or large muffin tin – it should hold about a 220ml volume of water. (Reserve and re-roll scraps.) Take the remaining quarter of the pastry and roll out to 3–4mm thick. Cut eight tops that will fit over your chosen muffin tin shape. Remember to cut a large hole in each top to fill with pesto after baking. Keep pastry cases and lids refrigerated until needed.

For the filling, mix the chicken, pork, bacon, onion, garlic, herbs and lemon zest in a large bowl. Season with salt and pepper to taste and refrigerate until required.

Remove the pastry cases and lids from the refrigerator. Divide the chicken and pork mixture between the cases, then brush rims with water. Take the pastry lids and cover the tops of the pies, pressing edges to seal, and trimming with a sharp knife. Transfer to a baking paper-lined oven tray and refrigerate until chilled (1 hour).

Remove pies from the refrigerator and brush the pastry with egg wash. Bake in a preheated 200°C (gas mark 6) oven for 45–50 minutes or until the pastry is crisp and golden-brown in colour.

Once at room temperature, spoon the rocket pesto into the holes in the pie lids and serve with Pear Mostarda.

Hearty Tamarillo Bourguignon Pie

This pie has a classic filling with a twist – it includes tamarillo (or *tree tomato*, as it is commonly referred to around the world). Wrapped up in a Smoked Paprika and Black Sesame Seed Puff Pastry, it is an all-year-round pie that is delicious served with a simple green salad.

MAKES A 20CM ROUND DEEP PIE, SERVING 6 PEOPLE

PASTRY

1 quantity of Smoked Paprika and Black Sesame Seed Puff Pastry (see page 206)

FILLING

2 tbsp oil

1 tbsp butter

800g braising beef (chuck), trimmed of excess fat and cut into 2.5cm chunks

4 slices bacon, cut into strips

1 onion, finely chopped

1 carrot, chopped into small cubes

salt and freshly ground black pepper, to taste

2 tbsp finely chopped rosemary

2 tbsp finely chopped thyme

2 tbsp plain flour

1 tbsp tomato purée

2 tbsp brown sugar

2 bay leaves

400ml red wine

5 tamarillos, peeled and halved, or vine-ripened tomatoes

4 cloves garlic, crushed

GLAZE

1 egg beaten with 1 tbsp water, for egg wash

½ tbsp sesame seeds

Make Smoked Paprika and Black Sesame Seed Puff Pastry ahead and rest it as required. Divide pastry into two portions (two-thirds for the base and one-third for the top). On a lightly floured surface, roll out the larger portion to approximately 3mm thick to line a 20cm round pie dish (5cm deep). Lightly oil the pie dish and line with the pastry, allowing a little to overhang.

Roll out the remaining pastry for the top of the pie into a 32cm-diameter circle, so it's just larger than the pie dish. Place on a baking paper-lined oven tray. Refrigerate the pastry base and top until chilled (30 minutes).

Heat the oil and butter in a large frying pan. Fry the beef in small batches for 2–3 minutes or until browned all over. Once the meat is browned, remove from heat and set aside.

Sauté the bacon, onion and carrot in a medium frying pan over a medium-high heat until soft and then add to the beef. Place the pan with the beef back on the element and season to taste. Add rosemary and thyme and then sprinkle with flour. Stir in the tomato purée, brown sugar and bay leaves. Add red wine, then cook, covered, over medium-low heat for about 1 hour. Add tamarillos and garlic, then return to the heat for a further 30 minutes until meat is tender. Set aside to cool.

Remove the pastry base from the refrigerator and transfer the filling to the lined pie dish. Drape remaining pastry over the pie dish and press down the edges to seal together.

Brush pastry with egg wash, sprinkle with sesame seeds and then make three slits in the top to allow steam to escape during baking.

Bake in a preheated 200°C (gas mark 6) oven for 30 minutes or until the pastry is crisp and golden-brown in colour.

Serve immediately with a fresh salad or seasonal vegetables.

Chicken, Sweet Potato and Stilton Pot Pies

**These comforting pies are creamy, cheesy and packed with hearty sweet
potatoes and chicken. Stilton gives a nice balance of flavour, but
if you don't have Stilton, then a good strong Cheddar will also be fine.
Serve with green vegetables cooked *al dente* and lightly seasoned with salt.**

MAKES 4 INDIVIDUAL PIES

PASTRY
½ quantity of Black Sesame Seed
Short Pastry (see page 198)

FILLING
1 red onion, finely sliced
4 cloves garlic, finely chopped
3 tbsp olive oil
6 skinless, boneless chicken
thighs, cut into medium chunks
salt and pepper, to season
2 tbsp standard plain flour, plus
extra for dusting
2 medium golden sweet potatoes,
cut into 1cm chunks
2 tsp finely chopped rosemary
20g flat-leaf parsley, finely
chopped
400ml chicken stock, hot
60ml double cream
150g Stilton, crumbled

GLAZE
1 egg beaten with 1 tbsp water,
for egg wash

Make a full quantity of Black Sesame Seed Short Pastry ahead and
rest it as required. Use half and put the rest into the freezer for
later use.

Divide the pastry into 4 equal pieces and then, on a lightly floured
surface, roll out until slightly larger than the tops of 4 × 350ml pie
dishes, to approximately 4mm thick. Lightly dust each disc with
flour, put between clingfilm, cover and place in the refrigerator
until required.

In a large saucepan over a medium heat, gently fry the onion and
garlic in 2 tbsp olive oil until softened, and then remove to a bowl.
Season the chicken with salt and pepper, roll in the plain flour,
then add to the pan with the remaining olive oil. Increase the heat
and fry until golden-brown on all sides.

Return the onion and garlic to the pan along with the sweet
potato, rosemary, parsley and chicken stock. Season and simmer
for 5 minutes. Remove from the heat, then stir through the cream
and Stilton.

Divide the filling equally between the pie dishes and allow to cool
(30 minutes).

Once the filling has cooled, remove the pastry lids from the
refrigerator, wet the edges of the pie dishes with water and place
a pastry lid on each dish. Press down firmly on the pastry with
your fingertips to seal and, using a sharp knife, trim off any excess
pastry hanging over the edges.

Brush the tops of the pastry with egg wash then, using a small
knife, cut two slits in the top of each to allow steam to escape
during baking.

Preheat the oven to 200°C (gas mark 6). Put a baking tray in the
oven to heat for 10 minutes. Place pies on tray and bake for 20–25
minutes or until the pastry is crisp and golden-brown in colour.

Bacon, Curried Egg and Ricotta Pie

**This is a big-flavoured twist on the beloved bacon and egg pie.
You won't be able to stop at eating just one slice!**

MAKES A 22CM ROUND DEEP PIE, SERVING 8–10 PEOPLE

PASTRY
1 quantity of Butter Puff Pastry
(see page 203)

FILLING
1 tbsp cumin seeds
80g Cheddar
10 slices streaky bacon, rind
removed
12 eggs
2 tsp curry powder
150g ricotta
20g flat-leaf parsley, finely
chopped
20g basil, finely chopped
salt and freshly ground black
pepper, to taste
150g sweet cherry tomatoes,
halved

GLAZE
1 egg beaten with 1 tbsp water,
for egg wash

Make Butter Puff Pastry ahead and rest it as required. On a lightly floured surface, roll out the pastry to approximately 3mm thick to line a 22cm, 5cm deep round pie dish (or a 22cm round cake tin with high sides). Lightly oil the pie dish and line with pastry, allowing some to overhang. Place in the refrigerator to chill whilst you are making the filling.

In a small dry saucepan over a medium heat, toast the cumin seeds until fragrant (1–2 minutes), shaking the pan every 30 seconds to prevent burning them. Set aside to cool slightly.

Remove pie dish from refrigerator. Grate the cheese and scatter over the base. Cut the bacon into long thin strips and place over the grated cheese in an even layer. Break in the eggs one at a time directly on top of the bacon. Run a knife through the eggs so the yolks just break – they should have a swirly effect. Mix the curry powder with the ricotta in a small bowl and dollop tablespoonfuls evenly over the eggs. Scatter the chopped herbs and toasted cumin seeds over top. Season generously with salt and freshly ground black pepper. Lastly place the halved cherry tomatoes on top.

Fold the excess pastry inwards, towards the middle of the pie, but not totally covering it. Brush the pastry edges with egg wash.

Bake in a preheated 200°C (gas mark 6) oven for 50 minutes or until the pastry is crisp and golden-brown in colour. Serve warm with spicy mango chutney.

Coriander Chicken and Yoghurt Curry Pie

The flavours of India predominate in this pie. The secret to its success is to marinate the chicken for as many hours as possible. Serve the pie piping hot with a lovely crisp salad and spicy mango dressing.

MAKES A 27CM PIE, SERVING 8 PEOPLE

PASTRY
1 quantity of Butter Puff Pastry
(see page 203)

MARINADE
30g fresh ginger
8 cloves garlic, peeled
300g thick plain yoghurt
4 tsp ground coriander
1 tsp garam masala
2 tsp salt
1 tsp ground cumin
pinch of turmeric

FILLING
800g boneless, skinless chicken
thighs, cut into 2.5cm chunks
2 tbsp vegetable oil
1 small onion, finely chopped
1–2 red chillies, seeded and
chopped
1 tbsp tomato purée
3 cardamom pods, seeds removed
and crushed
1 cinnamon stick
100ml double cream
1 large bunch coriander, leaves
and stalks finely chopped
2 tsp lemon juice
salt and pepper, to taste

GLAZE
1 egg beaten with 1 tbsp water,
for egg wash

Make Butter Puff Pastry ahead and rest it as required. Divide pastry into two portions (two-thirds for base and one-third for top). On a lightly floured surface, roll out larger portion to approximately 3mm thick to line a 27cm round pie dish (3cm deep). Lightly oil pie dish and line with pastry, allowing a little overhang.

Roll out the remaining pastry for the top of the pie into a 32cm-diameter circle, just larger than the pie dish. Place on a baking paper-lined oven tray. Refrigerate the pastry base and top until chilled (30 minutes). From any leftover pastry cut out decorations to place around the edge of the top (wrap in plastic to prevent drying out whilst preparing the filling).

In a small blender, purée the ginger and garlic with 200g of the yoghurt to make a smooth paste. Stir in the coriander, garam masala, salt, cumin and turmeric. Place the chicken in a bowl or a sealable container and stir in the marinade. Cover and leave in the refrigerator for a minimum of 2 hours or overnight.

Heat the oil in a large saucepan over a medium heat. Gently fry the onion and chilli until soft (5 minutes). Add the tomato purée and cardamom seeds and cook for another minute.

Add the cinnamon stick, then pour the chicken, marinade and the remaining 100g yoghurt into the saucepan and turn up the heat, cooking until the watery curry becomes creamy and covers a third of the chicken (10–15 minutes).

Reduce the heat to low and add the cream. Cover and cook for another 10 minutes, stirring occasionally. Add the coriander, lemon juice and seasoning to taste, then set aside to cool.

Take pastry from the refrigerator and spoon the curry mixture into the lined pie dish. Brush the rim of the pastry case with egg wash then drape the remaining pastry over the pie dish. Trim, then press the pastry edges firmly together to seal.

Brush the pastry with egg wash. Place the small pastry decorations around the edge of the pie and make four slits in the top to allow steam to escape during baking. Bake in a preheated 200°C (gas mark 6) oven for 30–40 minutes or until pastry is crisp and golden-brown in colour.

Sweet 'n' Spicy Veal, Pork and Macadamia Nut Tart

This tart is delicious served hot or warm, garnished with fresh mint leaves or rocket.

MAKES A 27CM TART, SERVING 8 PEOPLE

PASTRY
½ quantity of Fennel Pastry (see page 199)

FILLING
80g macadamia nuts
6 tbsp olive oil
350g veal mince
350g pork mince
3 tbsp tomato purée
2 tsp sugar
salt and pepper, to taste
1 tbsp dried mint
2 tsp ground allspice
1 tsp ground cinnamon
½ tsp ground nutmeg
1 tsp sweet paprika
½ tsp chilli flakes
2 onions, thinly sliced
4 cloves garlic, crushed
50g Parmesan, grated
7 free-range eggs
1 small handful mint leaves or rocket, to garnish

Make a half-quantity of Fennel Pastry ahead and rest it as required. Roll out the pastry on a lightly floured surface to 3mm thick, then grease and line a 27cm round, loose-bottomed tart tin, trimming the edges. Refrigerate for 1 hour. Line the pastry with aluminium foil and baking blind material and then bake blind (see page 214) in a preheated 180°C (gas mark 4) oven for 10 minutes. Remove foil and weights and bake until dry and crisp (10 minutes). Transfer to a rack to cool completely, about 30 minutes.

Spread macadamia nuts on a baking paper-lined oven tray and roast for 6–8 minutes until golden. Allow to cool slightly, then roughly chop.

To make the filling, heat half the olive oil in a large heavy saucepan over a medium-high heat. Add the veal mince. Break it up with a fork and cook it over a high heat for a few minutes to get some colour. Add the pork mince, mix well with a fork and keep on cooking over a medium heat for 15 minutes or until golden. Stir in the tomato purée and sugar and cook for a further 3 minutes. Add salt, pepper, mint and all the spices. Cook for a further 10 minutes over low heat.

In a separate pan fry the onions with the remaining olive oil until golden-brown, about 8 minutes. Add the garlic to the onions after 5 minutes of cooking. Be careful not to burn. Drain most of the oil and add the onion and garlic mixture and Parmesan to the cooked meat. Add the macadamia nuts and adjust seasoning as required.

To assemble the pie, spoon half of the cooled meat mixture into the pastry case. Make some shallow holes in the mixture and break in 3 of the eggs, one by one, pouring them into the holes. Using a wooden spoon, stir the eggs gently in the meat – just enough to disperse them a little, while keeping areas with more egg and maintaining some distinction between white and yolk. Spoon the rest of the meat on top, create some gaps and holes in it and break in the rest of the eggs, dispersing them as before.

Bake in a preheated 190°C (gas mark 5) oven for about 15 minutes or until the eggs are set. If the top begins to darken, cover it with aluminium foil for the remaining cooking period. Add garnish just before serving.

Chicken, Cranberry and Camembert Pies

**The first time I tasted this Christmas-time combination was at a
gourmet pizzeria, then it made its way into a gourmet burger and now it's
become famous in a pie – it was only a matter of time! The Olive Butter Puff Pastry
cuts through all the sweetness and creaminess.**

MAKES 4 INDIVIDUAL PIES

PASTRY
1 quantity of Olive Butter Puff
Pastry (see page 207)

FILLING
1 tbsp olive oil
1 clove garlic, finely chopped
350g chicken breast, skinned
and diced
50g butter
50g standard plain flour
400ml milk
1 tsp yellow or black mustard
seeds
¼ tsp freshly ground black
pepper
½ tsp salt
¼ tsp freshly ground nutmeg
1 tsp dried mixed herbs
8 tsp cranberry sauce
4 good slices of Camembert

GLAZE
1 egg beaten with 2 tbsp water,
for egg wash

Make Olive Butter Puff Pastry the day before and store, wrapped,
in the refrigerator. The chicken filling can also be made the day
before.

In a frying pan, heat a little olive oil and cook the garlic until soft,
then add the diced chicken to cook in its own juices. Drain any
excess juices and set aside until the sauce is ready.

Place the butter into a saucepan and melt over a medium heat, then
add the flour to the pan. Using a wooden spoon, blend the mixture
until a firm paste is formed. Slowly add the milk in small quantities,
mixing in each addition thoroughly to prevent lumps from forming.
Once all the milk is added, stir in the cooked chicken, mustard
seeds, pepper, salt, nutmeg and mixed herbs. Cover and set aside
until required.

Divide the pastry into two portions (three-quarters for the bases and
one-quarter for the tops). On a lightly floured surface, roll out the
larger piece of pastry to a square, approximately 4mm thick. Cut
the square into quarters. Line each individual pie dish, ensuring the
pastry is firmly pressed against the sides and leaving some hanging
over the edge. Roll out the smaller piece of pastry to a square,
approximately 3mm thick. Cut the square into quarters, cover with
clingfilm and set aside.

Fill each pastry-lined dish almost up to the top with the chicken
filling, then add cranberry sauce and place a slice of Camembert
on top.

Wash the edge of the pastry bases with water and place the lids on
top. Seal edges and trim off any excess pastry with a sharp knife.
Cut two slits in the top of each pie using a sharp knife and brush
the tops with egg wash. Rest for 1–2 hours (or longer) before baking.

Bake in a preheated 220°C (gas mark 7) oven for 25–30 minutes
until golden-brown in colour. Allow to cool in the dishes for 10
minutes, then remove from the dishes and place on a cooling rack.

Individual Beef Wellingtons

The trick to achieving a perfectly baked Beef Wellington is not to overcook the meat before cooling and wrapping in a delicate puff pastry. The mushrooms, Gorgonzola and truffle oil make a wonderful marriage with the beef. These pies go well with a simple, creamy potato mash and green beans.

MAKES 4 INDIVIDUAL PIES

PASTRY
1 quantity of Butter Puff Pastry
(see page 203)

FILLING
4 × 3.5cm-thick centre-cut beef
eye fillets
salt and pepper
1 tbsp butter
2 tbsp truffle oil
4 large mushrooms, thinly sliced
1 shallot, finely chopped
4 cloves garlic, finely chopped
4 tbsp Gorgonzola

GLAZE
1 egg beaten with 1 tbsp water,
for egg wash

Make Butter Puff Pastry ahead and rest it as required.

Preheat oven to 220°C (gas mark 7). Season beef with salt and pepper. In a shallow roasting pan, roast the fillets in the middle of the oven for 10 minutes, then cool (fillets will be baked again after being wrapped in pastry). Alternatively, cook the beef in a frying pan over a high heat searing it for 1–2 minutes on each side and ends. Cover and place in the refrigerator until cold, about 1 hour.

In a heavy saucepan, melt butter and truffle oil over a low-medium heat. Add mushrooms, shallot and garlic, and cook, stirring, until mushrooms are lightly browned. Season with salt and pepper, then transfer to a bowl to cool completely.

On a lightly floured surface, roll out pastry into a 35cm square, then cut into four equal pieces.

Put 1 tablespoon Gorgonzola in the centre of each pastry square and top with one-quarter of the mushroom mixture. Top with a beef fillet, pressing it down gently. Wrap two opposite corners of puff pastry over the fillet, overlapping them. Seal seam with egg wash. Wrap remaining two corners of pastry over fillet and seal in same manner. Seal any gaps with egg wash and press pastry around fillet to enclose completely. Arrange each Beef Wellington, seam-side down, on a non-stick baking tray. Chill, loosely covered, for at least 1 hour and up to one day.

Cut two slits in the top of each pie using a sharp knife and brush with egg wash just before baking.

Bake in a preheated 220°C (gas mark 7) oven for 20 minutes or until the pastry is crisp and golden-brown in colour.

Melton Mowbray-style Pork Pies

Serious pork pie followers will know of the Melton Mowbray Pork Pie. I was lucky enough to get a pork pie lesson from the managing director, Stephen Hallam, of Dickenson and Morris 'Ye Olde Pork Pie Shoppe'. Here is my version with one change . . . I have cheated with the jelly (but for those purists, I have included a pork pie jelly recipe on page 210)! Warning: these little delicacies are a 48-hour-plus process. You can make and bake them within a day, but the results will not be as good. Enjoy chilled with Stilton cheese and chutney.

MAKES 4 MEDIUM PIES

PASTRY
1 quantity of Hot Water Pastry
(see page 200)

PORK JELLY
500ml shop-bought pork stock
3 tsp powdered gelatine (or
6 sheets leaf gelatine, softened
in cold water)

FILLING
500g pork shoulder, finely
chopped into 5mm cubes
100g pork belly, skin removed,
minced
55g lean bacon, finely chopped
½ tsp freshly grated nutmeg
salt and freshly ground black
pepper

GLAZE
1 egg beaten with 1 tbsp water,
for egg wash

Make Hot Water Pastry the day before.

Heat the pork stock until it is almost boiling, then stir in the gelatine. Set aside overnight in the refrigerator. Warm to a liquid prior to using.

For the pie filling, place the pork, pork belly, bacon and nutmeg in a large bowl and mix well with your hands. Season with salt and freshly ground black pepper. Cover with clingfilm and set aside in the refrigerator overnight.

Take the pastry balls out of the refrigerator and manipulate one large ball at a time with your hands to soften it, to form a 6cm-round circle.

Once the pastry is soft, take one ball at a time and lightly dust the work surface with flour. Press a flour-dusted dolly (small jam jar, approximately 6.5cm in diameter) into the pastry circle until you feel it hit the bottom and the outer edges rise naturally. Use your right thumb and fingers to raise the pastry up the side of the dolly, turning it constantly with your left hand, pressing, pushing and raising the pastry up the sides of the jar until it's about 8cm in height. Gently slide your thumb between the pastry and the jar, slowly rotating the jar until the pastry case releases itself and comes away, leaving a pastry cup.

On a floured surface, roll out the smaller pastry balls to approximately 9cm-diameter circles, enough to cover each pastry case and filling as a lid. Cover with clingfilm and set aside.

Continues overleaf

Divide the pork pie filling into four equal portions, roll into balls and place one inside each pastry case.

Brush the top inner parts of each pastry casing with some of the egg wash and place the pastry lids on top. Pinch the edges of the pastry to seal each pie, then push the pastry top edges inwards between your thumb and forefinger to create a crimped wavy top edge. Cut two pencil-sized holes in the top of each one, brush with the rest of the egg wash, then place the pies on a tray and put uncovered in the refrigerator overnight. This helps set the pastry.

The following day, remove the pies and place them on a baking paper-lined oven tray. Bake in a preheated oven set at 230°C (gas mark 8) for 15 minutes, then reduce the heat to 190°C (gas mark 5) and bake for a further 1 hour 15 minutes or until the pies are a dark golden-brown all over.

Remove the pies from the oven and set aside to cool for 30 minutes. You may have to re-cut the small holes in the top in order to pour in the pork jelly through a cone made from non-stick baking paper (you will need to heat the jelly gently to loosen it for pouring). Chill the pies in the refrigerator until the jelly is set.

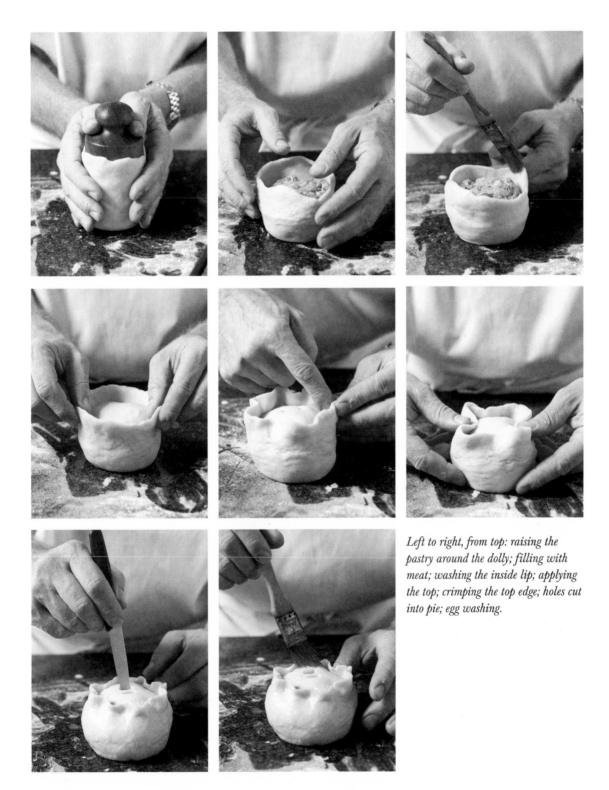

Left to right, from top: raising the pastry around the dolly; filling with meat; washing the inside lip; applying the top; crimping the top edge; holes cut into pie; egg washing.

Smoked Paprika, Chicken and Bean Pot Pies

**I love these little chicken pot pies. They remind me of the spicy
Chicken Hot Pots I ate on freezing nights in Shanghai; however, to these
I have added a Mexican chilli bean kick plus the spicy, crunchy texture of
a polenta pastry top for a little bit of extra bite.**

MAKES 4 × 500ML OR 6 × 350ML DISHES

PASTRY

1 quantity of Chilli Polenta Pie Crust (see page 199)

FILLING

2 tbsp sunflower oil

4 large chicken breasts, skin removed, cut into 2cm cubes

1 large onion, finely chopped

2 cloves garlic, finely chopped

1 tsp ground cumin

1 tbsp smoked paprika

200g chorizo sausage, cut into 1.5cm pieces

1 small red chilli, deseeded and finely chopped

1 red pepper, deseeded and diced

400g tin chopped tomatoes

400g tin kidney beans in brine

salt and pepper, to taste

GLAZE

1 egg beaten with 1 tbsp water, for egg wash

Make Chilli Polenta Pie Crust ahead and rest it as required. Divide the pastry into four or six equal pieces and then, on a lightly floured surface, roll out each piece until slightly larger than the tops of the pie dishes, ensuring the pastry is approximately 4mm thick. Lightly dust each lid with flour, put between clingfilm, cover and place in the refrigerator until required.

In a large saucepan, heat the oil over a medium heat until very hot. Add the chicken and cook until browned all over. You may need to cook the chicken in two batches. Remove and set aside on a plate.

Add the onion to the saucepan, reducing the heat, and cook for approximately 5 minutes until softened. Stir in the garlic, cumin, paprika and chorizo and cook for a few more minutes, then add the chilli and red pepper. Stir to combine. Add the tomatoes and kidney beans, then the browned chicken. Stir well and cook for a further 2 minutes, taking care not to overcook the chicken as you want it to remain in whole pieces. Season with salt and pepper to taste. Set aside to cool for 10 minutes, then spoon evenly into each dish and allow to cool.

Once the filling has cooled, remove the pastry lids from the refrigerator, wet the edges of the pie dishes with water and place a pastry lid on each dish. Press down firmly on the pastry with your fingertips to seal and, using a sharp knife, trim off any excess pastry. Using the back of a fork dipped in flour, press down on the edges to create a crimped pattern.

Brush the top of each pie with egg wash and then, using a small knife, cut two slits in the top of each to allow the steam to escape during baking.

Preheat oven to 200°C (gas mark 6) and put a baking tray in the oven to heat for 10 minutes. Place pies on tray and bake for 20–25 minutes or until the pastry is crisp and golden-brown in colour.

Gourmet Fruit-topped Pork Pies

These little gems remind me of traditional Cornish pasties. They are a real treat with the sharpness of the cranberry or apple filling on top of a traditional pork pie. They are good to eat on their own, and make a fantastic starter with a simple fresh green salad and pint of apple cider.

MAKES 8 SMALL PIES

PASTRY
1 quantity of Hot Water Pastry (see page 200)
melted butter, for greasing

FRUIT FILLING
1 quantity of Spiced Apple Filling (see page 210)
1 quantity of Cranberry Filling (see page 210)

PIE FILLING
500g pork shoulder, finely chopped into 5mm cubes
55g pork belly, skin removed, minced
55g lean bacon, finely chopped
½ tsp freshly grated nutmeg
salt and freshly ground black pepper

Make the Hot Water Pastry the day before and divide into eight equal-sized balls. Prepare the fruit fillings the day before making the pies.

For the pie filling, place the pork, pork belly, bacon and nutmeg into a large bowl and mix well with your hands. Season with salt and freshly ground black pepper. Cover with clingfilm and set aside in the refrigerator overnight.

Use eight small rings, 7cm in diameter and 4cm high. Alternatively, use a medium-sized muffin tray. Grease the rings or muffin cups with melted butter.

Take the pastry balls from the refrigerator and manipulate the balls with your hands to soften them. On a floured surface, roll out each ball in a circle, approximately 15cm in diameter and 3mm thick.

Line the rings or muffin cups with pastry, ensuring the pastry is pushed firmly into the bottom corners, then trim the top off level.

Divide the pork pie filling into eight equal portions and roll into balls. One at a time, press the balls firmly into the pastry cases, ensuring there is approximately 5mm of the pastry raised above the filling. Place each pork pie on a tray and leave uncovered in the refrigerator overnight. This helps set the pastry.

The following day, remove the pork pies and place them on a baking paper-lined oven tray. Allow to come to room temperature before baking.

Bake in a preheated oven set at 230°C (gas mark 8) for 15 minutes, then reduce the heat to 190°C (gas mark 5) and bake for a further 45 minutes. Remove from the oven and spoon a good tablespoonful of the prepared apple or cranberry filling over the filling in each pork pie and return to the oven for a further 15 minutes.

Remove the pies from the oven and set aside to cool for 15 minutes before removing from the rings or muffin cups. Serve warm, or cold from the refrigerator.

Seafood Pies

Fish Pie with Leek and Chorizo

A rising star in the baking world is Louise Wroth, the development chef at
Lantmännen Unibake UK. She is such a pleasure to work with and has a refreshing
mind when it comes to bringing cooking and baking together. When I asked
Louise for her favourite family pie recipe, she came up with this to add
to your list of family favourites.

MAKES A 600ML PIE DISH, SERVING 6 PEOPLE

PASTRY
½ quantity of Butter Puff Pastry
(see page 203)

FILLING
1 tbsp sunflower oil
1 leek, finely chopped
75g chorizo sausage, peeled and
chopped into small cubes
20g butter
20g standard plain flour
500ml milk
15g capers in brine, well washed
30g gherkins, finely chopped
bunch of flat-leaf parsley,
chopped
250g white fish, such as cod or
haddock, skinned and de-boned,
cut into bite-sized pieces
150g cooked peeled prawns

GLAZE
1 egg beaten with 1 tbsp water,
for egg wash

Make a half-quantity of Butter Puff Pastry ahead and rest it as
required.

In a large saucepan, heat the oil over a medium heat, then add the
leek and cook until softened. Add the chorizo and fry gently over
a low heat for 1–2 minutes until the chorizo flavours are released
into the pan. Remove the pan from the heat and use a spatula to
carefully remove all the leek and chorizo filling onto a plate to cool.
Set aside.

Using the same pan, add butter and melt over a very low heat then
add flour. Stir to a paste with a wooden spoon. Slowly add the milk
(a little at a time), stirring, to make a white sauce. Cook over a very
low heat until the sauce is bubbling and free from lumps.

Take the sauce off the heat and allow to cool in the pan. During this
time, roll out the pastry lid to fit the shape of the pie dish. Put the
rolled out pastry on a tray and place in the refrigerator to rest for
15–20 minutes while the sauce continues to cool down.

To the cooled sauce add the capers, gherkins, parsley, fish and
prawns, as well as the cooled leek and chorizo mixture. Stir gently to
distribute the ingredients through the sauce. Pour into the pie dish.

Remove the pastry lid from the refrigerator, wet the edges of the
pie dish with water and place the pastry lid on the dish. Press down
firmly on the pastry with your fingertips to seal and, using a sharp
knife, trim off any excess pastry. Using the back of a fork dipped in
flour, press down on the edges to create a crimped pattern.

Roll out the pastry offcuts. Cut out little fish shapes and place on
top of the pie to decorate. Brush the top of the pastry with egg wash
and then, using a small knife, cut two slits in the top to allow steam
to escape during baking.

Bake in a preheated 220°C (gas mark 7) oven for 20–25 minutes or
until the pastry is crisp and golden-brown in colour.

Smoked Salmon and Fennel Savoury Tart

Smoked salmon has always been a favourite of mine when it comes to savoury tarts and quiches. The distinct aniseed flavour of this tart balances the strong salmon flavour and the buttery crispness of the pastry. It will go beautifully with a fresh rocket salad and balsamic dressing. Serve it hot in winter and cold in summer. Keeping the pastry thin and par-baking it blind before filling prevents a thick, soggy pastry base.

MAKES A 20CM TART OR A 35CM × 10CM TART, SERVING 8 AS A STARTER AND 4 AS A MAIN

PASTRY
½ quantity of Basic Short Pastry (see page 197)

SAVOURY CUSTARD MIXTURE AND FILLING
50g soured cream
3 eggs
100ml double cream
freshly grated nutmeg
150g smoked salmon, diced
100g leeks, lightly cooked in butter and seasoned with salt and pepper
75g fennel, lightly cooked in butter and seasoned with salt and pepper
50g cream cheese
6 cherry tomatoes, sliced into halves
roughly chopped dill or thyme

Make Basic Short Pastry (Brisée Pastry) ahead, cover with clingfilm and place in the refrigerator to rest it as required.

On a lightly floured surface, roll out the pastry to form a sheet about 4mm thick and large enough to cover a greased 20cm fluted loose-bottomed flan ring (2.5cm deep) or a greased 35cm × 10cm fluted loose-bottomed tart tin (2.5cm deep).

Use the rolling pin to pick up the pastry and lay it over the ring or tin. Gently press the pastry into the tin so that it fills all the contours. Chill in the refrigerator for 30 minutes.

Preheat oven to 200°C (gas mark 6). Line the pastry with foil and fill with baking blind material. Bake blind (see page 214) for 20–25 minutes until it is lightly coloured. Remove the foil and weights. Lower the oven temperature to 180°C (gas mark 4).

To make the savoury custard mixture, place the soured cream into a mixing bowl and whisk by hand until smooth, then whisk in the eggs. Pour in the cream and a good sprinkle of grated nutmeg, then whisk to combine. Do not over-whisk at this stage otherwise the mixture will become too fluffy.

Toss the smoked salmon, cooked leeks and fennel together in a bowl to combine, then arrange in the pre-baked pastry case in a rustic fashion.

Pour the savoury custard mixture evenly into the case, taking care not to spill any mixture over the sides. Dot half teaspoonfuls of cream cheese and slices of tomato randomly over top of the filling and then evenly sprinkle with dill or thyme.

Bake in the preheated oven for 20–25 minutes or until the mixture is just set and firm to the touch. Do not over-bake. Allow to cool before removing from the flan ring or tart tin.

Snapper, Scallop and Chervil Pies

Making the effort to use Spinach Puff Pastry has two rewards – it creates colour and it adds an element of healthiness to the pies. Serve immediately with fresh spinach and walnut salad and hand-cut fries.

MAKES 4 INDIVIDUAL PIES

PASTRY
1 quantity of Spinach Puff Pastry (see page 206)

FILLING
75g butter
2 tbsp olive oil
8 scallops, roe removed, sliced in half
400g fresh snapper, cut into 1.5cm pieces
2 shallots, finely diced
½ leek, white part only, finely diced
100ml Chardonnay (or strong-flavoured white wine)
90ml fish stock
100ml double cream
4 tbsp chopped chervil
sea salt and freshly ground black pepper, to taste

GLAZE
1 egg beaten with 1 tbsp water, for egg wash

Make Spinach Puff Pastry ahead and rest it as required. Divide the pastry into four equal portions, then divide each portion again into two (two-thirds for the bases and one-third for the tops). On a lightly floured surface, roll out the four pastry bases to approximately 3mm thick to line four 10cm round pie dishes (3 cm deep). Lightly oil the pie dishes and line with pastry, allowing a little overhang.

Roll out the remaining pastry into 11cm-diameter circles for the lids, so they're just larger than the pie dishes. Place on a baking paper-lined oven tray. Refrigerate the four bases and tops until chilled (30 minutes).

Heat half the butter and the olive oil in a large saucepan over a medium-high heat until foaming. Add the scallops and snapper pieces and fry for 20 seconds. Remove from the pan and set aside on a plate. Add the remaining butter, and the shallots and leek to the same pan and fry for 3–4 minutes over a medium heat. Remove and set aside on a plate.

Deglaze the pan with the Chardonnay and cook until the liquid has reduced by half. Add the fish stock and cook for 1 further minute. Add the cream and bring the mixture to the boil (approximately 1 minute). Remove from the heat, then stir in the chervil and season with salt and pepper. Let the sauce cool slightly then transfer to a bowl with the scallops, snapper and leek. Mix all the ingredients together.

Remove pastry from the refrigerator and divide the mixture between the four lined pie dishes. Drape a pastry lid over each dish and press down the edges to seal them together.

Brush the pastry with egg wash, score a decorative pattern on top with the back of a knife and then make three slits in the top to allow the steam to escape during baking.

Bake in a preheated 220°C (gas mark 7) oven for 20 minutes or until the pastry is crisp and golden-brown in colour.

Salmon, Wild Rocket and Orzo Pie

This free-form creation is not a pie in the true sense but similar to a Russian fish pie with rice. A delicious combination of fresh salmon, pasta, lemon zest and feta, it is a perfect centrepiece for entertaining. You can devour it immediately or bake from frozen.

MAKES A LARGE PIE, SERVING 6 PEOPLE

PASTRY
1 quantity of Butter Puff Pastry (see page 203)

FILLING
700g piece of fresh salmon, skin and bones removed
150g wild rocket leaves
4 tbsp olive oil
120g chopped pancetta
1 onion, finely chopped
6 cloves garlic, peeled and finely chopped
8 anchovy fillets
sea salt and freshly ground black pepper, to taste
140g orzo pasta
zest and juice of 2 lemons
200g feta, crumbled
40g flat-leaf parsley, roughly chopped

GLAZE
1 egg beaten with 1 tbsp water, for egg wash

Make Butter Puff Pastry ahead and rest it as required. On a lightly floured surface, roll out pastry to form a rectangle, approximately 5mm thick and the same length as the piece of salmon. Place the pastry on a baking paper-lined oven tray and refrigerate until chilled (30 minutes).

Bring a medium saucepan of water to the boil over a high heat. Add rocket and blanch for 1 minute, then drop into a bowl of ice-cold water to refresh. Drain, then squeeze out excess water and finely chop.

Heat half the olive oil in a frying pan over a medium heat. Add pancetta and onion and stir occasionally until soft (8–10 minutes). Add garlic and anchovies; stir until anchovies melt (1–2 minutes). Transfer to a bowl to cool slightly and then add rocket. Season with salt and pepper and set aside until required.

To cook the orzo pasta, boil water in a large saucepan over a medium-high heat, add a generous pinch of salt and cook pasta until *al dente* (10 minutes). Drain the orzo, return it to the pan and add lemon zest and juice, feta, the remaining olive oil and chopped parsley. Season to taste with salt and pepper.

Arrange orzo mix in an even layer lengthways along centre of rolled puff pastry. Sit salmon on top then place the rocket mix on top of the salmon. Brush one long edge of pastry with egg wash. With longest side facing you, roll pastry over to form a cylinder, joining longest sides together and rolling so seam lies underneath. You can use any excess pastry to create a lattice pattern on the top, or simply brush pastry with egg wash, score the top with a knife to create portions and allow steam to escape. Chill for at least 10 minutes.

Bake in a preheated 230°C (gas mark 8) oven for 20–30 minutes or until the pastry is crisp and golden-brown in colour. Serve immediately with a fresh salad.

Spicy Monkfish Pies

The combination of roasted peppers, chorizo, olive, tomato and spice gives these pies a Moroccan feel.

MAKES 6 INDIVIDUAL PIES

PASTRY

1 quantity of Smoked Paprika and Black Sesame Seed Puff Pastry (see page 206)

FILLING

500g monkfish (or any meaty white fish i.e. cod, halibut), skin and bones removed, cut into 3cm cubes

2 tbsp flour, seasoned with a pinch of salt and pepper

25g butter

2 tbsp olive oil

6 cloves garlic, finely chopped

2 tsp Moroccan seasoning

2 tsp dried oregano

300g chorizo sausage, chopped into small chunks

salt and white pepper, to taste

400g tin chopped tomatoes in juice

200g jar sweet roasted peppers, roughly chopped

80g black pitted olives, roughly chopped

3 tbsp cream cheese

1 large bunch flat-leaf parsley, finely chopped

50g Parmesan, grated

juice of ½ lemon

2 tbsp extra virgin olive oil, for drizzling

GLAZE

1 egg beaten with 1 tbsp water, for egg wash

Make Smoked Paprika and Black Sesame Seed Puff Pastry ahead and rest it as required. Divide pastry into two portions (two-thirds for bases and one-third for tops). On a lightly floured surface, roll out each of the larger portions to approximately 3mm thick to line six individual pie dishes. Lightly oil the pie dishes and line with pastry, allowing a little overhang.

Roll the remaining pastry for the tops of the pies into six circles just larger than the pie dishes. Place on a baking tray with the pastry bases and refrigerate until chilled (30 minutes).

Place the fish in a bowl, add seasoned flour and toss a few times to coat the fish. Heat the butter in a large saucepan over a medium-high heat until foaming. Add the fish and fry for 20 seconds on each side, then remove from the pan and set aside on a plate.

Add olive oil to the saucepan, reduce the heat and add the garlic, gently frying for 1 minute. Turn the heat up to medium and add the Moroccan seasoning, oregano and chorizo, then season with salt and pepper and stir for another minute. Pour in the tomatoes and reduce the liquid by half (10–15 minutes).

Remove from the heat and transfer mixture to a bowl. Stir in roasted peppers, olives, cream cheese, parsley and Parmesan. Add lemon juice and extra virgin olive oil. Season to taste, then leave to cool slightly (approximately 30 minutes).

Take pastry from the refrigerator and spoon the mixture into your lined pie dishes. Brush the rims of the pastry cases with egg wash then drape the remaining pastry circles over the pie dishes. Trim, then press the pastry edges firmly together to seal. Crimp the rims with a fork dipped in flour.

Brush the pastry with egg wash, then make four slits in the top of each pie to allow the steam to escape during baking. Bake in a preheated 220°C (gas mark 7) oven for 35 minutes or until the pastry is crisp and golden-brown in colour.

Vegetarian Pies

Mushroom, Gouda and Goat's Cheese Galettes

These small tarts are a snack in themselves or they can be served with an accompanying roast vegetable and pumpkin salad as a summer lunchtime treat. They are simple and quick to make, even more so if you buy shop-bought puff pastry.

MAKES 12 INDIVIDUAL GALETTES

PASTRY
½ quantity of Butter Puff Pastry (see page 203)

FILLING
50g butter, chopped
4 shallots, finely chopped
3 cloves garlic, finely chopped
250g ricotta
50g Gouda, grated
40g grated Parmesan
3 tbsp each finely chopped marjoram, thyme and flat-leaf parsley
zest and juice of 1 lemon
1 egg yolk
sea salt and pepper, to taste
250g mixed mushrooms, sliced
100g rocket leaves
200g goat's cheese
extra virgin olive oil, to drizzle

GLAZE
1 egg beaten with 1 tbsp water, for egg wash

Make a half-quantity of Butter Puff Pastry ahead of time and rest it as required. (Or you could make a full quantity and keep the other half in the freezer for future use.) On a lightly floured surface, roll out puff pastry to approximately 4mm thick. Cut out twelve 10cm × 10cm pastry squares and place on a baking tray lined with non-stick baking paper. Using the back of a knife, score a border of 1 cm around the edge of each square. Set aside and cover with clingfilm.

Melt half the butter in a small saucepan over a medium heat, add shallots and garlic and sauté until tender (2–3 minutes). Transfer to a bowl and combine with the cheeses, herbs, lemon zest and juice, and egg yolk. Season to taste, then evenly top each pastry square with the ricotta cheese mixture keeping it inside the inner square.

Melt remaining butter in a small saucepan over a medium heat. Remove from the heat, then season with sea salt and pepper. Add the mushrooms and cook for 2–3 minutes until soft, then set aside and cool. Scatter mushrooms over ricotta cheese mixture. Brush edges of pastry with egg wash.

Bake in a preheated 220°C (gas mark 7) oven for 20–25 minutes or until crisp and golden in colour. Cool a little and then dress each pastry square with rocket leaves. Evenly crumble over the goat's cheese, and drizzle with olive oil. Serve warm or cold.

Asparagus, Lemon and Savoury Custard Tart

This is a simple quiche-style tart. The lemon and asparagus make a great partnership with the sautéed leeks and tarragon. It's so simple to make and is delicious with a rocket salad and a glass of lightly chilled Pinot Gris.

MAKES A 35CM × 10CM PIE, SERVING 6–8 PEOPLE

PASTRY
½ quantity of Basic Short Pastry (see page 197)

FILLING
½ medium leek (white and pale green parts only)
500g asparagus spears, trimmed (if fresh asparagus is unavailable tinned will be fine)
1 tbsp butter
salt and freshly ground black pepper, to taste
300ml double cream
2 eggs
zest of 2 lemons
20g flat-leaf parsley, finely chopped
2 tsp finely chopped tarragon

Make a half-quantity of Basic Short Pastry ahead of time and rest it as required. Roll out the pastry on a lightly floured surface to 3mm thick and use to line a 35cm × 10cm rectangular loose-bottomed tart tin, trimming the edges. Refrigerate for 30 minutes while you make the filling.

Wash the leek, then pat dry and chop into 5mm rounds.

Place the asparagus in a wide saucepan of boiling, salted water and cook, uncovered, until just tender (4–5 minutes). Transfer the asparagus with tongs to a bowl of ice-cold water to stop cooking, then drain and pat dry. Trim the asparagus stalks to fit the inside width of the tart tin.

Heat the butter in a large saucepan over a moderately low heat until foam subsides, then cook the leek with a pinch of salt and pepper, stirring until softened (approximately 6 minutes). Remove from the heat.

Whisk together the cream, eggs, lemon zest, parsley, tarragon, and salt and pepper. Spoon the cooked leek into the pastry shell, spreading evenly, then pour over the cream mixture. Lastly arrange the asparagus down the length of the tin.

Bake in a preheated 190°C (gas mark 5) oven for 40–45 minutes or until the filling is golden and just set but still slightly wobbly in the centre; the filling will continue to set as it cools.

Place tart on a cooling rack for about 30 minutes. Loosen the edges with a small sharp knife, then remove the tart tin. Serve warm or at room temperature, cut into slices.

Tomato and Thyme Tarte Tatin

**This is just as simple to make as the better-known apple tarte tatin.
I love serving it with a simple green salad with lots of
freshly picked basil leaves dressed with vinaigrette.**

MAKES A 20–22CM ROUND TART, SERVING 4 PEOPLE

PASTRY
½ quantity of Olive Butter Puff
Pastry (see page 207)

FILLING
12 medium vine-ripe tomatoes
handful of fresh thyme sprigs,
leaves picked, plus extra to serve
2 tbsp aged balsamic vinegar
50g Parmesan, finely grated

Make a half quantity of Olive Butter Puff Pastry in advance and
rest it as required. (Or you could make a whole quantity, use half
and wrap the remaining half in clingfilm and place in the freezer
for later use.) On a lightly floured surface, roll out pastry to 30cm
square, approximately 3mm in thickness. From this cut out a
rough circle a little wider than the top of a 20–22 cm heavy-based,
ovenproof frying pan. Discard the leftover pastry.

Place the whole tomatoes in a bowl and mix them with the thyme
leaves, then position evenly in the frying pan. Drizzle with the
balsamic vinegar and scatter over any thyme leaves left in the bowl.

Sprinkle half the Parmesan over the tomatoes, then top with the
pastry circle, tucking the edges well in around the inside of the
frying plan. Using a sharp knife, stab the pastry several times to
allow the steam to escape. Sprinkle with the remaining cheese.

Bake in a preheated 220°C (gas mark 7) oven for 20–25 minutes
or until the pastry is golden-brown and crispy. Allow to stand for
a couple of minutes before inverting the pan onto a plate. Add the
extra thyme sprigs and serve with a crisp salad.

Wholemeal Spinach, Feta and Potato Pies

I love these little purses. Spinach with feta is a classic combination, and the addition of potato and wholemeal pastry make these pies a little more satisfying. Be creative and add your own touches, be it sweet Thai chilli sauce, garlic or even caraway seeds.

MAKES 6 INDIVIDUAL PIES

PASTRY
140g plain wholemeal flour
140g standard plain flour, plus extra for dusting
85g cold butter, diced
85g shredded vegetable suet
100ml milk

FILLING
1 small baking potato, peeled and cut into small chunks
200g spinach
100ml double cream
100g feta, crumbled
1 egg, beaten
100g Cheddar, grated
salt and pepper
grated fresh nutmeg

GLAZE
1 egg beaten with 1 tbsp water, for egg wash

To make the pastry, rub the flours together with the butter and suet until it is the texture of breadcrumbs, then work in the milk (you may not need it all) until the pastry comes together. Knead the pastry on a bench until soft. Press the pastry into a flat, round shape and chill for 1 hour while you make the filling.

Boil the potato for 10 minutes until cooked, then drain. To wilt the spinach, tip it into a colander, pour over boiling water from a kettle, drain, then squeeze out all of the liquid. In a bowl, mix the spinach with the potato, cream, feta, egg and two-thirds of the Cheddar. Season with salt, pepper and nutmeg, then set aside.

Roll out the pastry on a floured surface to 3mm thick and cut out six squares, each approximately 13cm × 13cm. Spoon some mix into the centre of each square, then brush the edges with egg wash. Bring all four corners together over the filling, pinching the edges together to make a sealed purse with the pinched edges facing up.

Transfer the pies to a baking tray. Cut two slits in the top of each pie with a sharp knife. Brush each generously with egg wash, then top with a large pinch of grated Cheddar.

Bake in a preheated 220°C (gas mark 7) oven for 30 minutes or until golden and the cheese topping has melted. Leave to cool slightly. These are delicious warm but perfectly acceptable cold, too.

Gooey Leek, Potato and Vintage Cheddar Pie

This is almost a potato gratin in a pie, comprising layers of gooey leek, potato slices and Cheddar cheese. Take your time to create the layers, bake well and serve warm with a crisp salad on a lovely spring day.

MAKES A 22CM PIE, SERVING 6 PEOPLE

PASTRY
1 quantity of Toasted Walnut Short Pastry (see page 198)

FILLING
4 medium waxy potatoes, peeled and thinly sliced
2 tbsp olive oil
1 tbsp butter
4 large leeks, cleaned, halved lengthways and chopped into large pieces
salt and pepper, to taste
4 cloves garlic, finely chopped
350ml soured cream
2 large eggs, lightly beaten
2 tbsp wholegrain mustard
180g vintage Cheddar, grated
1 bunch chives, finely chopped
1 bunch flat-leaf parsley, finely chopped

Make Toasted Walnut Short Pastry ahead and rest it as required. On a lightly floured surface, roll out to approximately 3mm thick to line a 22cm spring-form cake tin (5.5cm deep). Lightly oil the tin, then line with pastry, trimming it 2cm from the top of the tin. Place into the refrigerator to chill.

Bring a medium saucepan of water to the boil, add the sliced potatoes and cook for 3–4 minutes until beginning to soften. Drain well and set aside.

Heat the oil and butter in a large saucepan over a medium-high heat. Add the chopped leek, season with salt and pepper and cook for 2–3 minutes. Add the garlic and cook for a further 3 minutes. Remove the pan from the heat and leave the leeks and garlic to cool slightly (15 minutes).

Mix together in a large bowl the soured cream, eggs, mustard, most of the Cheddar (reserving about 4 tablespoons for the top), the chives, parsley and a good pinch of salt. Stir in the cooled leeks and garlic.

Remove the pastry-lined tin from the refrigerator. Cover the base of the pie with a single layer of well-drained potato, then spoon the creamy leek mixture over the potato, repeating until both the potato and leek mixture is used up, with the last layer being the potato.

Place the pie into a preheated 190°C oven (gas mark 5) and bake for 40–45 minutes. Scatter the remaining Cheddar over the top and return to the oven for 5–10 minutes until it has turned golden in colour. The filling should still be gooey, but hold its shape when cut into wedges.

Slow-roasted Tomato and Herb Tartlets with Feta

These make great canapés or even small *amuse-bouche* when served with a lovely simple garlic aioli. Enjoy!

MAKES 24 TARTLETS

PASTRY
½ quantity of Basic Short Pastry (see page 197)

SLOW-ROASTED TOMATOES
12 large ripe cherry tomatoes
1 clove garlic, finely chopped
½ tbsp dried oregano
2 tbsp olive oil
sea salt and freshly ground black pepper, to taste

HERBY CHEESE FILLING
80g full-fat soft cheese with garlic and herbs (such as Boursin)
1 large egg, beaten
100ml double cream
4 tbsp very finely chopped fresh mixed herbs (such as parsley, basil, marjoram or chives)
sea salt and freshly ground black pepper, to taste
100g feta
tiny sprigs of thyme, to finish

Make a half-quantity of Basic Short Pastry and rest it as required. (Or make a whole quantity and keep the other half in the freezer for future use.) Bring the pastry to room temperature.

Roll out the pastry as thinly as possible on a lightly floured surface. Use a 6cm round cookie cutter to stamp out 24 circles. Line two 12-hole mini muffin trays with the pastry circles, then prick the bases and chill or freeze for 15 minutes. Line each pastry hole with aluminium foil and fill with baking blind material, then bake blind (see page 214) for 15 minutes in a preheated 200°C (gas mark 6) oven. Remove the foil and weights, allow to cool for 15 minutes then remove the baked pastry cases from the trays and let cool completely.

To make the Slow-roasted Tomatoes, turn down the oven to 170°C (gas mark 3). Cut the tomatoes in half around the middle. Arrange cut-side up on a baking tray. Put the garlic, oregano, olive oil and lots of sea salt and freshly ground pepper into a bowl and mix well. Spoon or brush over the cut tomatoes. Bake slowly for about 1 hour, checking every now and then. They should be slightly shrunken and still a brilliant red colour – if too dark, they will taste bitter.

Put the soft cheese into a bowl, add the egg, cream and chopped herbs and beat until smooth. Season well. Cut the feta into 24 small cubes.

When ready to bake, set the cases on a baking tray, put a cube of feta in each one and top up with the garlic and herb mixture.

Bake in a preheated 170°C (gas mark 3) oven for 15–20 minutes or until the filling is set. Top each tartlet with an oven-baked tomato half, drizzle with some of the tomato cooking juices and a thyme sprig. Serve warm or cold.

Swiss Chard, Squash and Ricotta Pithiviers

Traditionally, pithiviers are filled with an almond cream nestled on top of apricot jam, but a savoury filling will also taste delicious – just make sure you use one that will hold its shape. I use squash or pumpkin to bind everything together. Serve warm with mashed potato, your favourite gravy and lightly cooked garden vegetables.

MAKES 4 INDIVIDUAL PIES

PASTRY
1 quantity of Butter Puff Pastry (see page 203)

FILLING
1 large butternut squash, halved and seeds removed
50g butter
2 shallots, diced
2 small red chillies, deseeded and diced
1 tsp ground coriander
good pinch of nutmeg
100ml water
4 stalks Swiss chard, white stalks finely diced, greens shredded
100g ricotta
salt and pepper, to season

GLAZE
1 egg beaten with 1 tbsp water, for egg wash

Make Butter Puff Pastry in advance and rest it as required, preferably overnight in the refrigerator. On a lightly floured surface, roll out the pastry to 4mm thick and cut out eight discs, approximately 18cm in diameter. Lightly dust each disc with flour then put between clingfilm, cover and chill for 10 minutes (or several hours) in the refrigerator.

Place the two halves of butternut squash on a baking tray or in a roasting dish. Roast in a preheated 220°C (gas mark 7) oven for 30–40 minutes until the flesh is soft enough to scoop out. Scoop out the flesh into a bowl and mash with half of the butter. Set aside to cool.

Melt the remaining butter in a frying pan over a medium heat. Add the shallots, chilli, coriander and nutmeg. Fry for 10 minutes, add the water and the diced Swiss chard stalks, then increase the heat – as it cooks the water will evaporate.

Add the shredded green Swiss chard and stir-fry until wilted. Remove from the heat and cool. Stir in the ricotta. Season with salt and pepper and mix with the mashed squash. Set aside.

Remove the pastry discs from the refrigerator and place four of them onto a baking paper-lined oven tray and prick all over with a fork.

Divide the filling into four equal portions and put some mixture in the middle of each pastry disc in a big mound, allowing a 2cm rim of pastry around the outside. Brush the edges with water.

Place a pastry disc over each mound of filling, pressing down around it, getting rid of any air pockets.

Brush each pithivier with egg wash and then, using the back of a knife, start at the centre and mark curved lines until you have a spiral pattern all the way around. Poke a hole in the centre of each pastry top to allow steam to escape. Allow to rest for 30 minutes.

Bake in a preheated 220°C (gas mark 7) oven for 30–40 minutes or until crisp and golden.

Not-quite-a-pie

Pork, Prune and Sweet Apple Picnic Roll

This is essentially a huge sausage roll with the flavours of pork, prune, fennel, cheese and apple making for a lovely combination. Once you have had one slice, you can't help but go back for more. Make this to take to any family occasion where you know people will just want to tuck in. You can also make these into small rolls – just mix in the prunes with all the other ingredients.

MAKES A 14CM × 26CM ROLL, SERVING 8–10 PEOPLE

PASTRY
1 quantity of Butter Puff Pastry
(see page 203)

FILLING
2 shallots, peeled
1 bunch spring onions
1 large bunch flat-leaf parsley
2 tbsp thyme leaves
2 fennel bulbs
6 good quality pork sausages
2 sweet apples, grated and
squeezed of excess juice
2 tbsp wholegrain mustard
100g white breadcrumbs
125g soured cream
100g Cheddar cheese, grated
salt and freshly ground black
pepper
200g prunes

GLAZE
1 egg beaten with 1 tbsp water,
for egg wash
2 tsp fennel seeds

Make Butter Puff Pastry ahead and rest it as required. On a lightly floured surface, roll out puff pastry to a 45cm × 30cm rectangle, approximately 5mm thick. Place on a baking paper-lined oven tray and refrigerate until chilled (30 minutes).

Place shallots, spring onions, flat-leaf parsley, thyme and fennel bulbs in a food processor and blend until finely chopped.

Remove the skin from the sausages and place in a large bowl. Mix in the grated apple, mustard, breadcrumbs, soured cream, cheese and the blended shallot mixture, then season with a little salt and plenty of pepper. Take care not to over-salt as the sausages have already been seasoned.

Place half the sausage filling lengthways down the centre of the pastry and then arrange the prunes on top. Top with remaining filling and shape it to make a rectangle, approximately 14cm × 26cm.

Roll the pastry towards you making a long cylinder. Seal any joins and the ends with egg wash. Brush pastry with remaining egg wash, then score the top with a knife to create portions and allow steam to escape. Sprinkle with fennel seeds. Chill for at least 10 minutes.

Bake in a preheated 200°C oven (gas mark 6) for 1 hour or until the pastry is crisp and golden-brown in colour.

Once baked, rest for 10–15 minutes before slicing or wrap in aluminium foil and take for a picnic. Perfect with a crispy green salad.

Cornish Pasties

An everyday classic, these Cornish pasties feature a traditional pasty recipe for the pastry, but if you don't want to use lard, simply substitute it for butter or baking margarine. I even enlisted the help of someone from Cornwall to advise me on what vegetables to include. This is the outcome. If it's got any other ingredients, then it's not a proper pasty . . . or so I am told!

MAKES 4 LARGE DINNER-SIZE PASTIES

PASTRY
125g butter, chilled and diced
125g lard, diced
good pinch of salt
500g standard plain flour
5 tbsp cold water

FILLING
450g skirt or chuck steak, finely chopped
1 large onion, finely chopped
3 medium potatoes, peeled and thinly sliced
200g swede, peeled and finely diced
1 tsp freshly ground black pepper
1 tsp salt

GLAZE
1 egg, beaten

In a large mixing bowl, rub the butter, lard and salt into the flour with your fingertips until it resembles fine breadcrumbs. Mix in the cold water to make a firm dough. Knead for 2 minutes on a lightly floured surface. Cut into four equal pieces, mould each into a ball, cover with clingfilm and chill in the refrigerator for 20 minutes.

Mix together the filling ingredients in a large bowl and set aside.

Roll out each piece of dough on a lightly floured surface until large enough to make a 23cm-diameter circle – use a large dinner plate to trim it to shape.

Firmly pack a quarter of the filling in the centre of each circle. Brush the pasty all the way round the edge with beaten egg. Carefully draw up opposite sides so that they meet at the top, then pinch and crimp them together to seal. Lift the pasties onto a non-stick baking tray, cut two slits in the top of each pasty with a sharp knife and brush with the remaining egg to glaze.

Bake in a preheated 200°C (gas mark 6) oven for 10 minutes, then lower the heat to 180°C (gas mark 4) and bake for a further 45 minutes until golden. Great served warm with tomato sauce.

Chunky Chicken and Apricot Spinach Pastry Plaits

This refreshing twist on a sausage roll consists of spinach pastry enclosing a chicken filling stuffed with apricots, bacon and spring onions plaited to give it a special look. Serve warm, sliced, with a side salad and a glass of crisp cider.

MAKES 2 LARGE PLAITS, EACH SERVING TWO PEOPLE

PASTRY
1 quantity of Spinach Puff Pastry (see page 206)

FILLING
2 tbsp olive oil
1 clove garlic, finely chopped
1 small onion, finely chopped
100g streaky bacon, chopped
2 spring onions, finely chopped
300g minced chicken or finely chopped chicken breast
60g dried apricots, finely chopped
25g breadcrumbs
¼ tsp salt
a few good grinds of pepper

GLAZE
1 egg beaten with 2 tbsp water, for egg wash

Make Spinach Puff Pastry the day before and store wrapped in the refrigerator.

In a frying pan, heat the olive oil and add the garlic and onion. Fry over a medium heat until softened, but not coloured. Add the bacon and fry until cooked, then turn off the heat. Add the spring onions and mix to combine. Remove from the heat and set aside until cool.

Add the chicken, apricots, breadcrumbs, salt and pepper to the cooled bacon and onion mixture and, using your hands, forcefully mix thoroughly for 2–3 minutes to strengthen the chicken meat proteins and give the filling some structure. Cover and set aside in the refrigerator until needed, or overnight.

Divide the pastry into two equal parts. On a floured surface, roll each piece out to form a 20cm square, trimming the edges to make a perfect square.

Continues overleaf

 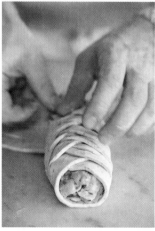 

Divide filling into two equal amounts then roll each one into an 18cm-long log shape. Set aside on a plate.

Using a sharp knife, cut seven 7cm-long strips on the diagonal on each piece of pastry from the outer edge inwards – they should be equal down each side of the pastry. Place the filling log in the centre. Pick up one strip at a time and fold it over the filling, alternating each side, so that you are encasing the filling by plaiting the strips of pastry over it (see photographs).

Place both plaited logs onto a baking paper-lined oven tray and brush the top and sides of each pastry plait with egg wash. For best results leave the prepared plaits to rest for 1 hour before baking.

Bake in a preheated 220°C (gas mark 7) oven for 20–25 minutes or until the pastry is golden-brown and crisp. Remove from the oven and stand for 5 minutes before serving.

Lamb, Harissa and Almond Sausage Rolls

Another sausage roll, this time with a North African character, using lamb combined with harissa paste and a touch of sweetness added by the currants. When eaten warm the caraway seed topping leaves a nice after-taste.

MAKES 20 ROLLS

PASTRY
1 quantity of Butter Puff Pastry
(see page 203)

FILLING
50g flaked almonds
1 shallot, finely chopped
1 clove garlic, crushed
600g minced lamb
100g harissa paste
40g couscous
65g currants
1 small egg
20g flat-leaf parsley, finely chopped
salt and pepper, to season

GLAZE
1 egg beaten with 1 tbsp water, for egg wash
1 tbsp caraway seeds, for sprinkling

Make Butter Puff Pastry ahead and rest it as required.

In a small dry saucepan over a medium heat, toast the almonds until golden (1–2 minutes), shaking the pan every 30 seconds to prevent them burning. Set aside to cool slightly.

Roughly chop the flaked almonds then add to a large mixing bowl with the shallot, garlic, lamb, harissa, couscous, currants, egg, parsley and salt and pepper. Using your hands, mix all the ingredients thoroughly. The couscous will bind the filling together.

On a lightly floured surface, roll out the puff pastry to a 3mm-thick rectangle. Using a piping bag with no nozzle, pipe the lamb mixture along the longest edge, then roll the pastry over to enclose. Brush egg wash along the pastry edge and press to seal. Trim along the length of pastry and repeat with remaining mixture and pastry until both are used up. Alternatively, if you have no piping bag, on a floured surface roll the lamb mixture in ropes 2.5cm thick, then place onto the pastry.

Using a large, sharp knife cut rolls into 5–6cm lengths and place onto a baking paper-lined oven tray. Brush the top of each roll with egg wash and sprinkle with caraway seeds. Rest for 30 minutes.

Bake in a preheated 220°C (gas mark 7) oven for 35 minutes or until the pastry is crisp and golden-brown in colour. Serve warm with spicy tomato chutney.

Onion and Bacon Flammkuchen

This pizza-style bread comes from the Alsace region of France, which borders Germany. There are many, many variations, but the traditional Alsace Flammkuchen is made with a *hefeteig* (yeasted dough) and is spread with crème fraîche and topped with diced bacon and sliced onions. Tomatoes and rosemary are added for more flavour as well as colour, for it is a very pale bread.

MAKES A 28CM PIE, SERVING 4 PEOPLE

DOUGH
100g bread flour
good pinch of salt
1½ tbsp olive oil
½ tsp fresh yeast (or ¼ tsp active dried yeast)
60ml warm water

TOPPING
150g thick crème fraîche
½ medium onion, sliced
70g diced bacon
3 cherry tomatoes, sliced
1 small sprig rosemary
salt and pepper
extra virgin olive oil

Place all the dough ingredients into a large mixing bowl. Using a wooden spoon, combine the ingredients until a dough mass has formed. Tip the dough out onto a lightly floured surface and knead for approximately 10 minutes (taking a rest period of 30 seconds, every 3–4 minutes) until the dough is smooth and elastic in feel. Lightly oil a bowl, then put the dough in it and cover with clingfilm. Leave in a warmish place (23–25°C) for 45 minutes to allow the dough to double in bulk. Gently knock back the dough in the bowl by gently folding it back onto itself until it resembles a round ball shape. Cover again with clingfilm and leave for 30 minutes.

Tip out the dough onto a lightly floured surface. Flatten the round dough ball with the palm of your hand and, using a rolling pin, roll out the dough to a 28cm-diameter circle. Place on a baking paper-lined oven tray.

Using the back of a tablespoon, spread a thick layer of crème fraîche over the base of the dough, right out towards the edges. Sprinkle with slices of onion and pieces of bacon. Arrange the cherry tomatoes evenly on the topping and toss a few rosemary leaves over. Season with salt and pepper, then lightly drizzle with olive oil.

Loosely cover the surface with a sheet of aluminium foil and rest for 20 minutes before baking.

Preheat oven to 240°C (gas mark 9) and place a baking tray on the middle shelf to heat up. If you have a pizza stone, place it in the oven 1 hour before required to ensure it is well heated.

Slide the Flammkuchen (with the baking paper underneath) directly onto the preheated baking tray or pizza stone and bake for approximately 10 minutes with the aluminium foil on. Remove the foil and bake for a further 5–8 minutes. Serve hot from the oven.

Cornish Pasties with Apple

This version of the good old Cornish pasty is a blast from the past, as they used to make them in the days of the Cornish tin miners. Legend suggests that burly Cornish men ate their pasties down in the depths of the mines and that the thick, rope-like edge of the pastry served as a handle for their big dirty hands. To balance out their diet, one end of the pastie was filled with meat, and the other with apple for dessert.

MAKES 4 SMALL PASTIES

PASTRY
2 quantities of Basic Short Pastry
(see page 197)

MEAT FILLING
200g rump steak, 1cm diced
125g onion, medium sliced
125g potato, peeled and 1cm diced
100g turnip or swede, peeled and 1cm diced
salt and pepper, to season

APPLE FILLING
2–3 small Granny Smith apples, peeled, cored and 1cm diced
1 tbsp sugar
juice of ½ lemon
¼ tsp cinnamon

GLAZE
1 egg beaten with 2 tbsp water, for egg wash

Make Basic Short Pastry the day before, divide into four equal-sized balls and store wrapped in the refrigerator. On a lightly floured surface, roll out each pastry ball to the size of a small lunch plate (20cm) 3–4mm thick. Cover with clingfilm and set aside in the refrigerator until later. Wrap any leftover pastry in plastic and keep in the freezer for another time.

To make the meat filling, mix all the ingredients together in a bowl, season with salt and pepper, cover and set aside.

To make the apple filling, mix all the ingredients together in a bowl, then cover and set aside.

Place the four pastry circles on the bench. Divide the meat filling into four equal portions and place some filling in the middle of each pastry circle, slightly off centre. Next, evenly divide the apple filling into four portions and place each one next to the meat filling. Using your hand, slightly flatten the two fillings.

Using a pastry brush, lightly dampen one half of each pastry circle's edge and fold it over to make a half moon or D-shape. Press firmly to seal the two edges together. From the right-hand side (or left, if you are left-handed), using your forefinger and thumb of both hands, fold, tuck and crimp the two edges together to form a kind of twisted-rope pattern along the edge. The seam should run along the top, but I find it easier to run it along the side.

Place the pasties on a baking paper-lined oven tray and, using a pastry brush, brush the entire pasty with egg wash. Make a hole in the top surface of each pasty with a sharp knife to allow steam to escape during baking. Rest the pasties for 30 minutes.

Bake in a preheated 200°C (gas mark 6) oven for 15 minutes, then turn the heat down to 180°C (gas mark 4) and bake for a further 15–20 minutes or until golden-brown in colour. Allow to cool before placing onto a cooling rack.

Classic Sausage Rolls

Jill Milburn and her students from the Aoraki Polytechnic in New Zealand shared this recipe with me. It's perfect for anyone's birthday party or after-match eats at the local rugby or football club. The breadcrumbs bake nice and crisp and the sausage rolls are delicious dipped in tomato sauce.

MAKES 15 ROLLS

PASTRY
1 quantity of Butter Puff Pastry (see page 203)

FILLING
350g sausagemeat
60g breadcrumbs
50ml water
1 medium onion, finely chopped
2 tbsp wholegrain mustard
2 good pinches of salt
¼ tsp freshly ground black pepper
1 good pinch of cayenne pepper

GLAZE
1 egg beaten with 1 tbsp water, for egg wash
50g breadcrumbs

Make Butter Puff Pastry ahead and rest it as required.

On a lightly floured surface, roll out the puff pastry to form a 3mm-thick rectangle.

Put sausagemeat, breadcrumbs, water, onion, mustard, salt and peppers into a bowl and mix with a wooden spoon until well combined. Cover with clingfilm and allow to sit for 20–30 minutes until the meat is rested and the mixture stiffens a little.

Place the sausagemeat mixture in a piping bag without a nozzle and pipe the sausagemeat mixture along the longest edge of the pastry. Roll the pastry over to enclose. Brush egg wash along the pastry edge and press to seal. Alternatively, if you don't have a piping bag, roll the sausagemeat on a floured surface in ropes 2.5cm thick, then place onto the pastry. Trim along the length of the pastry then repeat with remaining mixture and pastry. Cut into 6cm lengths.

Place sausage rolls seam-side down on a baking paper-lined tray. Brush each roll all over with egg wash and sprinkle with breadcrumbs. Allow to rest for 30 minutes before baking to prevent the pastry shrinking and the sausage rolls becoming misshapen.

Bake in a preheated 210–215°C (gas mark 6–7) oven for about 25–30 minutes or until golden-brown in colour.

Smoked Fish Empanadas

An empanada is a stuffed bread or pastry, baked or fried, which is made in Latin America, southern Europe and parts of south east Asia. The name comes from the verb *empañar*, meaning to wrap or coat in bread. The benefit of using a smoked fish filling, in this case haddock, is that you can eat it hot or cold as a snack.

MAKES 12 EMPANADAS

PASTRY
1 quantity of Basic Short Pastry (see page 197)

FILLING
500g aubergine
80g caster sugar
zest and juice of 2 lemons
3 cloves garlic, finely chopped
1 tbsp thyme leaves
60ml hazelnut oil
salt and pepper, to taste
400g smoked haddock (or any smoked fish)

GLAZE
1 egg beaten with 1 tbsp water, for egg wash

Make Basic Short Pastry ahead and rest it as required. On a lightly floured surface, roll out the pastry to approximately 3mm thick and then, using a 13–15cm saucer as a template, cut out discs of pastry just before you are ready to fill.

Preheat oven to 200°C (gas mark 6) and line a large baking tray with foil. Cut off both ends of the aubergines then peel their skins. Finely dice the flesh and place in a large bowl. Add in sugar, lemon zest and juice, garlic and thyme and toss to combine. Spread out on the prepared tray and cover with another piece of foil. Bake for 45–50 minutes, stirring the aubergine once or twice until it is very soft and lightly caramelised. Drain off any juices that may have formed during the cooking process.

Remove from the oven and transfer to a blender. Blend to a rough paste. With the motor still running, slowly pour in the hazelnut oil until the purée is smooth. Transfer the purée to a saucepan and cook over a high heat to dry it out slightly (2–3 minutes). Season well with salt and pepper to taste then allow to cool for 20 minutes.

Flake the fish into small pieces, then mix in the candied aubergine.

To fill the empanadas, place 2 heaped tablespoonfuls of the mixture on one half of each of the pastry circles. Brush the edge with egg wash, fold over and crimp the edges together with a fork dipped in flour. Brush the pastry with egg wash then, using a fork, poke holes into the tops to allow steam to escape.

Bake in a preheated 200°C (gas mark 6) oven for 10 minutes or until the pastry is crisp and golden-brown in colour.

Chocolate Whoopie Pies

There are many stories around the origins of Whoopie Pies, two cake-style discs sandwiched with a butter cream filling, but the fact that they are called 'Whoopie Pies' is why they are here. You can use any good-quality preserve, conserve or jam to replace the Blackberry Compote in the filling.

MAKES 20 INDIVIDUAL SERVES

BATTER
240g standard plain flour
70g unsweetened cocoa powder
1½ tsp bicarbonate of soda
¼ tsp salt
100g butter, softened
175g dark soft brown sugar
1 egg
1 tsp vanilla extract
260ml milk

BLACKBERRY COMPOTE
(Make the day before)
50g caster sugar
2 tbsp cold water
200g frozen blackberries (or blueberries)

VANILLA CREAM
200g cream cheese, at room temperature
50g butter, softened
140 g icing sugar, sifted, plus extra to serve
1 vanilla pod, sliced lengthways, seeds scraped out

Line two baking trays with non-stick baking paper and set aside.

To make the batter, sift together the flour, cocoa, bicarbonate of soda and salt into a bowl and set aside.

In an electric mixer, beat the butter and brown sugar until just combined and then increase the speed and beat until light and fluffy, pale in colour and smooth (about 3 minutes). Add the egg and vanilla extract and beat for another 2 minutes. Add half of the dry ingredients and half of the milk and beat on slow speed until just incorporated. Scrape down the sides of the bowl, then add the remaining dry ingredients and milk. Gently beat until completely combined.

Place the mixture into a piping bag fitted with a 1cm plain piping tube and pipe a tablespoon (approximately 20 grams) at a time of mixture onto the non-stick baking paper, spaced about 3cm apart.

Place one tray at a time into a preheated 180°C (gas mark 4) oven and bake for approximately 10 minutes or until the pies spring back when gently pressed with your finger. Cool on the baking paper and then remove gently and allow to cool completely before filling.

To make the Blackberry Compote, place sugar and water in a small saucepan over a low heat, stirring until sugar dissolves. Increase heat to high. Bring mixture to the boil. Cook for 3 minutes or until mixture thickens slightly. Remove from heat. Stir in berries. Set aside to cool completely.

To make the Vanilla Cream, place cream cheese in a medium bowl and beat with an electric mixer on high for 1 minute. Add butter, icing sugar and vanilla pod seeds and beat on high until smooth, about 3 minutes.

Continues overleaf

To assemble the pies, swirl together the vanilla cream and cooled compote then pipe or spread a rounded tablespoon of filling on the flat side of half the cakes. Top with remaining cakes. Sift icing sugar over cakes just before serving.

Fig and Goat's Cheese Tart

This large, family-sized tart makes a great table centrepiece. You can also make it into smaller individual tarts. Serve alongside a large bold tomato and bread salad with a sharp vinaigrette, or eat as a starter at a casual dinner party.

MAKES A 15CM × 40CM TART, SERVING 6 PEOPLE

PASTRY
1 quantity of Butter Puff Pastry
(see page 203)

PORT-SOAKED FIGS
150g dried figs, roughly chopped
120ml port
2 tbsp granulated sugar

FILLING
80g butter, melted
1 large red onion, finely chopped
4 cloves garlic, finely chopped
20g thyme, sage and rosemary
(combined), finely chopped
200g red seedless grapes
2 tbsp standard plain flour, sifted
3 tbsp olive oil, plus extra to
serve
salt and freshly ground black
pepper, to taste
120g crumbly goat's cheese
8 slices prosciutto
12 sage leaves
200g fresh figs, cut in quarters

GLAZE
1 egg beaten with 1 tbsp water,
for egg wash

Make Butter Puff Pastry ahead and rest it as required. On a lightly floured surface, roll out the pastry to form a 15cm × 40cm rectangle, approximately 5mm thick. Place on a baking tray lined with non-stick baking paper. Trim the edges to make them straight, then using the back of a sharp knife score a 2cm border all the way around. Brush the border with egg wash and then score it again to create a decorative effect. Chill pastry for 30 minutes.

Bring figs, port and sugar to the boil in a small saucepan over a high heat. Reduce the heat and simmer for 10 minutes or until port is absorbed. Allow to cool slightly.

To make the filling, heat half the butter in a medium saucepan over low heat. Add onion and garlic and sauté until tender (5–7 minutes). Add herbs and stir to combine, then set aside to cool. Combine grapes, soaked figs, flour, onion mixture and 1 tablespoon of olive oil in a bowl, seasoning to taste.

Spread filling over pastry, within the 2cm border, then scatter over the goat's cheese.

Bake in a preheated 200°C (gas mark 6) oven for 30–35 minutes or until the pastry is crisp and golden-brown in colour.

Meanwhile, heat the remaining olive oil in a large frying pan over high heat, add prosciutto and turn occasionally until crisp (3–4 minutes). Drain on a paper towel and set aside. Next heat the remaining butter until foaming, add sage leaves and fry until crisp (30–60 seconds). Remove with a slotted spoon, drain on a paper towel and set aside.

Remove the tart from the oven and scatter with sage, prosciutto and quartered figs. Drizzle with olive oil and season with freshly ground black pepper.

Spicy Gingerbread, Cointreau and Chocolate Eccles Cakes

Recently, a high-profile celebrity chef made Christmas fruit mince pies with puff pastry and pine needle icing sugar to sprinkle on after baking. When I tested them, I was disappointed to discover that the pine needle scent disappeared right after sprinkling. This spurred me into thinking how I would have made them, and here is the result – a gingerbread puff pastry encasing a spicy Eccles filling with a touch of chocolate and Cointreau. Delicious!

MAKES 9 ECCLES CAKES

PASTRY
1 quantity of Gingerbread Puff Pastry (see page 208)

FILLING
250g currants
100ml Cointreau
25g butter, softened
70g dark soft brown sugar
80g cake crumbs (any cake crumbs will do)
75g dark chocolate chips
30g golden syrup
½ tsp mixed spice
zest and juice of 1 lemon
200g caster sugar, for dipping

Make Gingerbread Puff Pastry ahead and rest it as required.

In a bowl, soak the currants with the Cointreau overnight to macerate and ensure the currants become plump and juicy. The next day, place the butter and brown sugar into a bowl and beat together with a wooden spoon until soft and creamy, but not light and fluffy. Add the macerated currants and remaining ingredients except the caster sugar, and mix until well combined. You may need to adjust the consistency by adding a few more cake crumbs until you have a soft but firm filling.

On a lightly floured surface, gently roll out the puff pastry to approximately 4mm thick and then cut into 9 × 10cm squares. Place one heaped tablespoon of the filling into the centre of each square. Using a pastry brush dipped in water, lightly brush the edges of each square and then bring each corner of pastry into the centre and pinch together, then gather in the remaining pastry and secure to completely enclose the filling.

Using the palm of your hand slightly flatten each pie and turn over so that the scrunched side is flat on the bench. Lightly roll out to achieve a 7–8cm-diameter circle. Brush the tops and sides with water and dip into caster sugar, ensuring an even coating. Arrange them on a baking paper-lined oven tray and cut two vent holes into the top of each one with a sharp knife. Allow the cakes to rest for at least 1 hour.

Bake in a preheated 210–220°C (gas mark 6–7) oven for approximately 20 minutes or until the sugar has become golden-brown and has just started to caramelise. Remove from the oven and allow to cool.

Strawberry, Raspberry and Rhubarb Shortcake

Shortcakes are from my grandmother's era and so are these faithful natural fillings. What a lovely combination, especially when served with a quality strawberry ice cream. A very comforting dessert or even afternoon tea treat.

MAKES A 20–22CM SHORTCAKE, SERVING 8 PEOPLE

FRUIT
3–4 stalks rhubarb
3 tbsp caster sugar
75g frozen strawberries (if using fresh strawberries, trim and slice)
65g frozen raspberries

SHORTCAKE
125g butter, softened
125g caster sugar
1 egg
225g standard plain flour
25g cornflour
1 tsp baking powder

Line the bottom of a 20–22cm, shallow, round, non-stick cake tin with baking paper.

Trim, wash and slice the rhubarb and put in a large non-stick frying pan with the sugar. Place over gentle heat, shaking the pan every now and then, until the fruit is almost tender. Add the frozen strawberries and raspberries to the pan, shake and set aside until lukewarm.

To make the shortcake, put the softened butter and sugar in a mixing bowl and beat until light and fluffy, then beat in the egg. Sift together the flour, cornflour and baking powder and beat until just mixed.

Scoop almost two-thirds of the dough into the cake tin and press it evenly over the bottom and up the sides (the remaining dough will be used for the topping). If you need to bake the shortcake immediately, spread the warm fruit over the shortcake base, and dab pinches of the shortcake dough over the top, allowing a little of the fruit to peep through. Or sprinkle flour on a piece of greaseproof paper, roll out the dough and flip it on top of the fruit. If the dough is very soft you can even use a piping bag to make a lattice pattern. If you have 20 minutes to spare, after lining the tin with dough set it aside unfilled. Then form the topping dough into a cylinder, wrap it in baking paper and put in the freezer until firm, about 20 minutes. Spread the cool fruit over the shortcake base and cut the chilled dough into discs. Arrange the discs in an overlapping pattern over the fruit.

Bake in a preheated 180°C (gas mark 4) oven for about 30 minutes or until the shortcake is a light biscuit brown. Remove from oven and allow to cool for a few minutes before turning out onto a cooling rack and then onto a plate. Serve warm or cold.

Date, Apricot, Orange and Cardamom Flapjack Shortcake Tart

This high-energy caramel and date-flavoured shortcake tart is loosely based on the Scottish oat flapjack, with the addition of seeds for nuttiness. Serve warm with a scoop of vanilla ice cream or eat cold as a wedge with a nice cup of coffee or tea.

MAKES AN 18CM TART, SERVING 4–6 PEOPLE

FILLING
150g dates, chopped
50g dried apricots, chopped
100ml orange juice
zest of 1 orange

SHORTCAKE
115g butter
¼ tsp vanilla extract
100g rolled oats, the large flat type, not instant or finely milled porridge oats
40g pumpkin seeds
40g sunflower seeds
100g standard plain flour or wholemeal flour
100g brown sugar
¼ tsp cinnamon
¼ tsp cardamom
30g egg (about ½ egg), whisked

Place all filling ingredients into a medium-sized saucepan and bring to the boil. Reduce the heat to medium and stir for 1 minute to break down the filling to form a paste-like consistency.

Set aside to cool slightly before using.

Grease and line the base of an 18cm round tart tin with non-stick baking paper.

To make the shortcake, melt butter in a microwave or saucepan. Add vanilla extract and set aside.

Combine oats, seeds, flour, brown sugar and spices in a medium-sized bowl and mix in melted butter and egg to combine.

Press half the shortcake mixture into the base of the tart tin and then cover with the fruit filling. Top with the remaining shortcake mixture, pressing together to seal, and form an even top layer.

Bake in a preheated 180°C (gas mark 4) oven for 30–35 minutes and then allow to cool completely before cutting into pieces. It is best left overnight to allow it to firm up completely.

Sweet Pies

Prune, Pine Nut and Pumpkin Pie

**The soft and fibrous texture of prunes allows them to blend with
the strong taste of the spiced pumpkin filling, while pine nuts give a unique
flavour. Serve with a rhubarb compote and whipped cream.**

MAKES A 20CM ROUND PIE, SERVING 8 PEOPLE

PASTRY
½ quantity of Basic Sweet Pastry
(see page 193)
1 egg beaten with 1 tbsp water,
for egg wash

PUMPKIN FILLING
250g pumpkin (cooked and
puréed in a blender or mashed
then pressed through a fine sieve)
50g light soft brown sugar
2 eggs
100g evaporated milk
pinch of salt
¼ tsp mixed spice
½ tsp ground cinnamon
few drops of vanilla extract
1 tbsp rum
100g soft eating prunes

ROASTED PINE NUTS
30g pine nuts

GLAZE
1 quantity of Apricot Glaze (see
page 209)

Make a half-quantity of Basic Sweet Pastry the day before and store wrapped in the refrigerator. (Alternatively, you can make the full recipe, use what you require and then wrap the rest in clingfilm and freeze for later use.) On a lightly floured surface, roll out the pastry to approximately 3mm thick and cut a circle slightly larger (approximately 23cm in diameter) than the 20cm flan ring in which it will be baked. Line the flan ring with the pastry and trim off the top edges with a sharp knife. Line the pastry with aluminium foil and fill with baking blind material. Set aside on a baking tray for at least 30 minutes to relax the pastry.

Bake blind (see page 214) in a preheated 180°C (gas mark 4) oven for approximately 20 minutes or until light golden-brown in colour. Remove the foil and weights and immediately brush with egg wash to seal the pastry case. Return to the oven and bake to set the egg wash, about 2 minutes.

Combine all the Pumpkin Filling ingredients except the prunes into a mixing bowl and, using a hand whisk, mix together until well combined and smooth. Don't over-whisk as you don't want too much air to be incorporated. Set aside.

Place the pine nuts in a heavy frying pan over a medium heat. Slowly roast in the pan, moving them all the time, until light amber in colour. Alternatively, place the pine nuts on a baking tray and roast in a preheated 150°C (gas mark 2) oven.

Pour the pumpkin filling into the baked pastry case, right up to the top. Insert the prunes evenly into the filling, ensuring they are covered, then sprinkle the top with the roasted pine nuts.

Bake in a preheated 170°C (gas mark 3) oven for 20–25 minutes or until filling has just set and is still a little wobbly. Cool before removing from the tin. Brush with hot Apricot Glaze and allow to set before cutting.

Apricot, Almond and Honey Tart

Traditionally the almond cream in this tart is made with sugar, but honey adds a natural sweetness and flavour that you don't get from normal white sugar. The pistachios not only create an eye-catching dessert, but also add another layer of intense flavour. Serve with a rich, creamy vanilla ice cream.

MAKES A 35CM × 10CM TART, SERVING 8 PEOPLE

PASTRY
1 quantity of Butter Puff Pastry
(see page 203)

**ALMOND AND HONEY
CREAM FILLING**
50g butter, softened
40g honey
1 egg, beaten
50g finely ground almonds
20g standard plain flour

APRICOT FILLING
10 small apricots

GLAZE
1 quantity of Apricot Glaze (see page 209)
20g pistachios, finely chopped

Make Butter Puff Pastry the day before and store wrapped in the refrigerator. When ready, roll out the Butter Puff Pastry on a floured surface to approximately 4mm thick to fit inside a greased 35cm × 10cm rectangular fluted flan or loose-bottomed tart tin. Line the tin with the pastry and trim the top edges with a sharp knife.

Place the butter and honey into a mixing bowl and, using a wooden spoon, cream until light and fluffy. Slowly add the egg and beat until combined, then beat in the ground almonds and flour. Cover and set aside until required.

Wash and dry the apricots. Cut each apricot in half, remove the stone and cut into quarters. Place in a bowl.

Fill the pastry base with a thin layer of Almond and Honey Cream, then arrange the apricots around the outside, cut side down, working inwards until the tart is well packed with fruit. Leave the tart to rest for 30–60 minutes.

Bake in a preheated 180°C (gas mark 4) oven for 30–35 minutes or until the fruit has turned dark at the edges and the filling is cooked. Brush with hot Apricot Glaze while still hot and sprinkle all over with chopped pistachios.

Mini Spiced Berry Cobblers

Sometimes small is good and these little cobblers, full of winter spice flavours combined with apple and mixed berries, are no exception. Serve them with a teaspoon of vanilla ice cream, which melts down through the crunchy crumble and into the hot fruit filling.

MAKES 6 MINI COBBLERS

SPICED BERRY FILLING
150ml red wine
good pinch of cinnamon
1 star anise
2 whole cloves
25g granulated sugar
zest of 1 orange
1 medium cooking apple, peeled, cored and cut into 5mm cubes
100g mixed berries (raspberries, blueberries, redcurrants, blackberries, strawberries), fresh or frozen
½ tsp cornflour mixed with 1 tsp cold water

CRUMBLE TOPPING
100g standard plain flour
30g rolled oats
pinch of salt
50g butter
50g brown sugar
30g walnuts, very finely chopped
¼ tsp cinnamon

Place the wine, cinnamon, star anise, cloves, sugar and orange zest into a saucepan over a medium heat and bring to the boil. Add the cubed apple and cook until tender, but not too soft. Add the mixed berries and simmer for a few minutes, stirring occasionally. Stir in the cornflour slurry and cook until thickened, then remove from the heat. Place in a bowl to cool and cover with clingfilm. This can be made a few days in advance and kept in the refrigerator. Remove the star anise and cloves before using.

To make the Crumble Topping, place the flour, oats and salt into a mixing bowl and, using your fingers, rub in the butter until the mixture resembles breadcrumbs. Mix in the sugar, walnuts and cinnamon. Set aside.

Spoon the fruit filling into six 100ml ramekins or ovenproof glasses and then pile on the Crumble Topping.

Bake in a preheated 180°C (gas mark 4) oven for 10 minutes until the crumble is light brown in colour. Serve warm.

Pear and Fennel Tarte Tatin

To shake things up completely, I've used Smoked Paprika and Black Sesame Seed
Puff Pastry here instead of plain puff pastry. The sweet smokiness of the paprika
gives a gentle warming after-taste as you experience the lovely pear and fennel-
infused caramel topping. Vanilla ice cream is a perfect fit with this.

MAKES A 20CM TART, SERVING 8 PEOPLE

PASTRY
¾ quantity of Smoked Paprika
and Black Sesame Seed Puff
Pastry (see page 206)

**PEAR, FENNEL AND
CARAMEL GLAZE**
6 medium-sized ripe pears
100g unsalted butter, softened
220g caster sugar
1 tbsp fennel seeds, lightly
bruised to release the flavour

Make Smoked Paprika and Black Sesame Seed Puff Pastry the
day before and store wrapped in the refrigerator. Remove the
pastry from the refrigerator and allow to sit for 20 minutes at room
temperature before using. On a lightly floured surface, roll out the
puff pastry to 4–5mm thick then, using a sharp knife, cut out a
circle (the size will depend on the size of your ovenproof frying pan).
Fold the pastry in half and then in half again to make a quarter,
wrap in clingfilm and place in the refrigerator.

Peel and core pears, then cut each one in half. In a bowl, mix
together the softened butter and sugar to form a soft batter-like
consistency.

Evenly coat the bottom of a 20cm ovenproof frying pan (or large,
heavy-based, round baking dish) with the softened butter and
sugar mixture. Sprinkle the fennel seeds evenly over the mixture,
then place the pear quarters on top, round-side down, in a circular
pattern, starting from the outside first and working your way into
the middle.

Place the frying pan over a low heat to allow the butter and sugar
mixture to dissolve and start to bubble. Shake the pan very gently to
ensure even cooking. When the caramel syrup is simmering evenly,
turn up the heat, and cook for 5–8 minutes or until the pears are
tender and the caramel syrup has thickened and turned golden-
brown. Occasionally, gently shake the pan to ensure even cooking.
Remove the frying pan from direct heat and allow to cool for
5 minutes.

Place the pre-rolled puff pastry circle on top of the pears, tucking
the edges of the pastry inside the rim of the frying pan or dish. Prick
with a fork or knife several times to allow the steam to escape and
prevent the pastry from doming.

Place the frying pan or dish into a preheated 220°C (gas mark 7)
oven and bake for 10 minutes. Reduce the heat to 200°C (gas

mark 6) and bake for a further 20–25 minutes or until the pastry is golden-brown and cooked through.

Carefully remove the baked tart from the oven and allow to cool for 3–4 minutes. Place a large, flat serving plate on top of the pastry and then, holding the plate and the pan firmly together, flip and invert so the plate is now on the bottom and the frying pan is on the top. Carefully remove the frying pan. Take extreme care when doing this, as the caramel syrup will still be runny and very hot.

Allow to cool slightly before cutting into eight wedges.

Dark Chocolate Banoffee Slab

I love a good banoffee (short for banana and toffee) pie. This one comes in a slab form, but it can be made in the round classic shape, too. The addition of the chocolate topping makes it even richer and totally indulgent. Serve with a good dollop of freshly whipped cream on a cold winter's night.

MAKES A 35CM × 10CM TART, SERVING 8 PEOPLE

PASTRY
½ quantity of Chocolate Sweet Pastry (see page 194)

FILLING
100g butter
160g golden syrup
395g tin sweetened condensed milk
2 bananas, sliced lengthways

TOPPING
225g dark chocolate, roughly chopped
50g butter
50g flaked almonds

TO SERVE
200g whipped cream

Make a half-quantity of Chocolate Sweet Pastry ahead and rest it as required. (Alternatively, you can make the full recipe, use what you require and then wrap the rest in clingfilm and freeze for later use.) Roll out 300g of the pastry on a lightly floured surface to 3mm thick and use it to line a 35cm × 10cm loose-bottomed tart tin, trimming the pastry edges. Refrigerate for 1 hour.

Line the pastry with aluminium foil, then fill with baking blind material. Bake blind (see page 214) in a preheated 180°C (gas mark 4) oven for 10 minutes, then remove foil and weights and bake until dry and crisp (10 minutes).

To make the caramel filling, place the butter, golden syrup and condensed milk into a heavy-based saucepan and cook over a low-medium heat, stirring, until thick and golden-brown. Remove from the heat and pour over the cooked base leaving a 7.5mm space from the top of the pastry. (Any caramel left over can be kept to drizzle over vanilla ice cream.)

Bake in a preheated 180°C (gas mark 4) oven for 15 minutes.

To make the topping, place chocolate and butter in a heatproof bowl over a saucepan of gently simmering water, not letting the bowl touch the water. Allow chocolate to melt, then stir until smooth. Remove from heat and cool slightly.

Place the sliced bananas over the cooked caramel and pour the melted chocolate over top, smoothing with a palette knife and sprinkling with flaked almonds.

Remove and cool completely before slicing into slabs. Serve with whipped cream.

Classic Tarte au Citron with Raspberry Coulis

This was the first dessert I learnt to make when I was training to become a pastry chef in London in 1990. The Lemon Crème Filling should be smooth and mellow in flavour, balanced out by the sharpness of the Raspberry Coulis.

MAKES A 20CM TART, SERVING 8 PEOPLE

PASTRY
½ quantity of Basic Short Pastry (see page 197)
1 egg beaten with 1 tbsp water, for egg wash

LEMON CRÈME FILLING
2 large lemons
4 eggs
90g caster sugar
150ml double cream

RASPBERRY COULIS
220g fresh or frozen raspberries
50g caster sugar, or to taste
lemon juice, to taste
crème fraîche, to garnish

Make Basic Short Pastry the day before and store wrapped in the refrigerator. (You can make the full recipe, use what you require and then wrap the rest in clingfilm and freeze for later use.) On a lightly floured surface, roll out the pastry to approximately 3mm thick and cut a circle slightly larger (approximately 23cm in diameter) than the 20cm flan ring in which it will be baked. Line the flan ring with pastry and trim off the top edges with a sharp knife. Line the pastry with aluminium foil and fill with baking blind material. Set aside on a baking tray for at least 30 minutes to relax the pastry.

Bake blind (see page 214) in a preheated 180°C (gas mark 4) oven for approximately 20 minutes or until light golden-brown in colour. Remove the foil and weights and brush immediately with egg wash to seal the pastry case. Return to the oven and bake to set the egg wash, about 2 minutes.

Wash the lemons in warm water. Zest the lemons and squeeze all the juice into a small bowl.

Combine the eggs and sugar in a bowl and gently mix together, then lightly whisk in the cream and lastly add the lemon zest and juice. Don't over-whisk as you don't want too much air to be incorporated. The mixture will look split at first, but it will become nice and smooth after the gentle mixing.

Place the raspberries into a saucepan and bring to the boil. Add the sugar and stir to dissolve. Place in a blender and purée, then strain into a small bowl through a very fine sieve to remove any seeds. Adjust the tartness by adding lemon juice to suit your taste. Cool until required.

Continues overleaf

Pour the Lemon Crème Filling into the baked pastry case, right up to the top, taking care not to spill any over the edges while transferring to the oven. A small trick is to fill the tart when it is already in the oven standing on the baking tray.

Bake in a preheated 150–160°C (gas mark 2–3) oven for about 20–25 minutes or until the filling has set. Cool before removing from the tin.

Cut into eight wedges and serve with crème fraîche and Raspberry Coulis.

Raspberry and Caramelised Apple Galette

Galette is French for a free-form tart. The secret of this simple dessert is to caramelise the apples well so their sweetness combines beautifully with the tart flavour of the raspberries and richness of the Toasted Walnut Short Pastry. Serve hot or cold with a vanilla ice cream.

MAKES A MEDIUM-SIZED GALETTE, SERVING 6 PEOPLE

PASTRY
1 quantity of Toasted Walnut Short Pastry (see page 198)

ALMOND CREAM FILLING
50g granulated sugar
50g butter, softened
1 egg
50g ground almonds

FRUIT FILLING
50g butter
3 tart apples, such as Granny Smith, peeled, cored and cut into 8 wedges
50g brown sugar
100g frozen raspberries

GLAZE
1 large egg beaten with 1 tbsp water, for egg wash

Make Toasted Walnut Short Pastry the day before, roll it into a ball shape, then press it flat and store wrapped in the refrigerator.

To make the Almond Cream Filling, beat the sugar and softened butter in a medium bowl with a wooden spoon until light and creamy in texture, then add the egg and beat in before adding the ground almonds. Beat for about 2 minutes until well combined. Scrape down the sides of the bowl, cover with clingfilm and set aside.

To make the fruit filling, melt the butter in a large non-stick frying pan over medium heat. When it's foamy, add the apples and stir frequently until slightly softened and browned at the edges (8–10 minutes). Sprinkle brown sugar over fruit and stir until liquid is syrupy and bubbling, about 5 minutes. Remove from the heat and gently stir in frozen raspberries so you don't break them up too much. Allow to cool.

Unwrap the pastry from the refrigerator and, on a lightly floured surface with a lightly floured rolling pin, roll into a 30cm-diameter circle. Carefully transfer pastry to a baking paper-lined tray.

To assemble, place about half of the Almond Cream in the middle of the pastry and level it out with the back of a spoon (the remaining cream can be frozen in an airtight container for future use). Pour apple and raspberry mixture onto the centre of the pastry, piling the wedges into a circle about 18cm in diameter and 5cm high. Gently fold edges of dough over the apples, pleating as you go, leaving an opening about 10cm wide in the centre. Brush pastry all over with egg wash.

Bake in a preheated 190–200°C (gas mark 5–6) oven for about 40–45 minutes or until the pastry is golden-brown and apples are tender when pierced. Allow to cool for 15 minutes on the baking tray, then transfer the baked galette to a cooling rack to cool.

Transfer to a large serving plate and serve.

Cranberry and Apple Cobbler

I have replaced the usual crumble topping with a cranberry scone, which is a great way to soak up all the natural juices. Dollop a generous spoonful of cobbler onto a pudding plate and serve with a good amount of lightly whipped pouring cream flavoured with vanilla extract and a little icing sugar.

MAKES A 25CM COBBLER, SERVING 6–8 PEOPLE

FRUIT FILLING
1kg cooking apples, such as Granny Smith or Bramley
350g frozen cranberries or mixed summer berries
zest and juice of 2 oranges
¼ tsp Chinese five spice powder
3 whole star anise

SCONE TOPPING
220g self-raising flour
good pinch of salt
55g caster sugar
55g butter, chilled
100g dried cranberries, roughly chopped
165ml milk

GLAZE
1 large egg beaten with 1 tbsp water, for egg wash

Peel, core and thickly slice the apples. Place in a large saucepan with the cranberries, orange zest and juice, Chinese five spice and star anise over a medium heat and very gently poach for approximately 15 minutes until tender. Remove from the heat and set aside to cool. Discard the star anise before using. This filling can be made a day in advance and kept in the refrigerator overnight.

To make the scone topping, place the flour, salt and sugar into a large bowl and rub in the butter with your fingertips until the mixture resembles fine breadcrumbs. Add the dried cranberries and toss through, then add the milk and mix with a wooden spoon or blunt knife to achieve a soft, sticky dough.

Tip out the dough onto a lightly floured surface and roll out to 2cm thick. Using a 5cm-round cookie cutter, cut out circles of dough and set aside.

Spoon the Fruit Filling into a 25cm shallow round, ovenproof baking dish and arrange the scone circles on top around the edge of the dish, slightly overlapping each other but leaving an open circular gap in the middle. Brush the circles with egg wash.

Bake in a preheated 220°C (gas mark 7) oven for 20–25 minutes or until the scone circles are golden-brown in colour.

Remove from the oven and allow to cool for 10 minutes on a cooling rack before serving.

Lemon, Olive Oil and Blueberry Tart

Lemon and blueberry are great partners as the lemon brings out the blueberry flavour. Adding olive oil makes the filling silky and highlights the gingerbread crust. If you don't like blueberries, you can substitute any fresh berries such as raspberries or strawberries.

MAKES A 27CM TART, SERVING 10–12 PEOPLE

PASTRY
½ quantity of Gingerbread Crust Sweet Pastry (see page 195)

FILLING
2 tbsp lemon zest
240ml lemon juice
200g caster sugar
2 tsp cornflour
2 large whole eggs
3 large egg yolks
140g unsalted butter, roughly chopped
3 tbsp fruity olive oil
200g fresh or frozen blueberries

GLAZE
1 quantity of Apricot Glaze (see page 209)
200g crème fraîche

Make a half-quantity of Gingerbread Crust Sweet Pastry ahead and rest it as required. (You can make the full recipe, use what you require and then wrap the rest in clingfilm and freeze for later use.) Roll out the pastry on a lightly floured surface to 3mm thick and line a 27cm round loose-bottomed tart tin, trimming the edges. Refrigerate for 1 hour.

Line the tart with aluminium foil and fill with baking blind material. Bake blind (see page 214) in a preheated 180°C (gas mark 4) oven for 10 minutes. Remove foil and weights and bake the shell until dry and crisp (10 minutes). Transfer to a rack to cool completely, about 30 minutes.

For the filling, whisk together lemon zest and juice, sugar, cornflour, whole eggs and yolks in a medium saucepan and bring to the boil over a medium heat, whisking constantly. Boil for 2 minutes, whisking constantly, until thick. Remove from the heat and whisk in butter and olive oil until smooth.

Pour lemon filling into cooled pastry case and scatter with blueberries. Pat blueberries down slightly with a spatula and chill until set, at least 2 hours. Brush with Apricot Glaze and slice into wedges. Serve with a dollop of crème fraîche.

Pecan Praline and Chocolate Tart

This rich, indulgent dessert bar is almost like Toblerone chocolate. Pecans, toffee and chocolate work so well together. Eat it on its own – it really doesn't need to be served with anything else.

MAKES A 35CM × 10CM TART, SERVING 8 PEOPLE

PASTRY
1 quantity of Chocolate Sweet Pastry (see page 194)

FILLING
100g pecan nuts
125g caster sugar
40ml cold water
200ml double cream
250g milk chocolate

GANACHE TOPPING
150ml double cream
150g dark chocolate

Make Chocolate Sweet Pastry ahead and rest it as required. Roll out 300g of the pastry (freeze the rest for future use) on a lightly floured surface to 3mm thick and use it to line a 35cm × 10cm loose-bottomed tart tin, trimming the edges. Refrigerate for 1 hour.

Line the tart with aluminium foil and fill with baking blind material. Bake blind (see page 214) in a preheated 180°C (gas mark 4) oven for 10 minutes. Remove foil and weights and bake the case until dry and crisp (10 minutes).

To make the filling, spread the pecan nuts on a baking paper-lined oven tray and roast in the preheated oven for 10 minutes. Mix sugar and water in a small saucepan and stir over a medium-high heat until the sugar dissolves. Bring to the boil, cook until caramel in colour (6–8 minutes), then pour over pecans. Stand until set (10 minutes), then blend in a food processor until roughly ground. Set aside until needed. Bring the cream to a simmer over a medium heat, add milk chocolate and stir until smooth. Remove from heat and stir in two-thirds of the praline mixture. Pour into the baked pastry case and refrigerate until set (1½ hours).

To make the Ganache Topping, bring the cream to a simmer in a small saucepan over a medium heat and add dark chocolate. Stir until smooth, then remove from heat. Remove the set tart from refrigerator, spread ganache over tart, and then sprinkle with any remaining praline. Refrigerate until topping is just set (approximately 1 hour).

Cut into slabs with a hot knife and serve immediately, and, if you must have something with it, a dollop of crème fraîche.

Caramel Macadamia Oaty Tart

This tart, which keeps well, is the ideal afternoon 'pick me up' as it's full of high-energy but indulgent caramel goodness. Cut it very thinly and enjoy with a hot cup of coffee or tea.

MAKES A 27CM TART, SERVING 10–12 PEOPLE

BASE
150g butter
100g brown sugar
1 tsp vanilla extract
200g standard plain flour
2 tsp baking powder

CARAMEL FILLING
130g macadamia nuts, roughly chopped
100g unsalted butter
160g golden syrup
600g sweetened condensed milk

TOPPING
140g rolled oats
50g shredded coconut
150g brown sugar
100g butter, melted

To make the base, beat together the butter and brown sugar until pale and creamy. Add vanilla, flour and baking powder and mix well. Press the mixture evenly over the bottom and up the sides of a baking paper-lined, 27cm round loose-bottomed round tin (3cm deep).

Bake in a preheated 180°C (gas mark 4) oven for 20 minutes or until golden.

Spread the macadamia nuts on a baking tray and toast in the preheated oven until a light amber colour. Take care as they will colour fast and continue to cook when you take them out of the oven. Set aside to cool.

To make the filling, place the butter, golden syrup and condensed milk into a heavy-based saucepan and cook over a low-medium heat, stirring, until thick and golden-brown. Remove from the heat and stir in the cooled macadamia nuts.

To make the topping, mix together the rolled oats, coconut, brown sugar and melted butter.

Spread the Caramel Filling over the cooked base and sprinkle rolled oat mixture on top.

Bake for 25 minutes in the preheated oven until golden in colour. Allow to cool completely before slicing.

Pecan Tarts

Making these little tarts is easy and they are great to serve as a dessert with vanilla ice cream. You can substitute pecans with good-quality walnuts, if you like. The syrup mixture will make a little more than you need, but it can be stored in an airtight container in the refrigerator for a week. Simply remove from the refrigerator and stir, then pour it into the tart cases and top with pecans.

MAKES 6–8 INDIVIDUAL TARTS

PASTRY
1 quantity of Basic Sweet Pastry
(see page 193)

FILLING
100g brown sugar
2 eggs
¼ tsp salt
¼ tsp vanilla extract
10g standard plain flour
200g liquid glucose (weigh by pouring from a jar or use a spoon dipped in water)
15g maple syrup
20g butter, melted
100g pecan pieces

GLAZE
1 quantity of Apricot Glaze (see page 209), optional

Make Basic Sweet Pastry ahead and rest it as required.

Place the brown sugar, eggs, salt, vanilla extract and flour into a mixing bowl and whisk by hand for 2 minutes. Add the liquid glucose and maple syrup and whisk gently until combined. Lastly whisk in the melted butter until evenly combined. Cover and set aside. This mixture will keep for up to a week in the refrigerator.

On a lightly floured surface, roll out the pastry to approximately 3mm thick. Cut 6–8 circles slightly larger than the tart tins in which they will be baked (approximately 10cm in diameter). Line the tart tins with the pastry and trim off the top edges with a sharp knife.

Using a small spoon, fill the sweet pastry-lined tart shells, approximately three-quarters full. Place pecan pieces on top.

Bake in a preheated 200°C (gas mark 6) oven for 20–25 minutes or until the tops and cases are lightly golden-brown in colour. Remove from the oven and cool for 10 minutes. Remove from the tins and brush with the hot Apricot Glaze if you wish.

Roast Pear and Blueberry Pie

Roasting any fleshy fruit with brown sugar is a lovely way to get the best out of the natural fruit sugars and the fruit in this pie is no exception. Combined with blueberries, a twist of lemon and a hint of cinnamon, this is a wonderful warming pie for a cold winter's night. Serve piping hot with loads of ice cream.

MAKES A MEDIUM-SIZED PIE, SERVING 4–6 PEOPLE

PASTRY
1 quantity of Soured Cream and Lemon Pastry (see page 195)

FILLING
6 ripe but firm pears, peeled, cored and cut into 2cm cubes
30g unsalted butter, melted
50g brown sugar
½ tsp cinnamon
juice of 1 lemon
200g blueberries

GLAZE
1 egg beaten with 1 tbsp water, for egg wash
1 tbsp Demerara sugar, for sprinkling

Make a quantity of Soured Cream and Lemon Pastry ahead and rest it as required. Divide pastry into two portions (two-thirds for base and one-third for top). On a lightly floured surface, roll out the larger portion to approximately 3mm thick to line a 22cm × 15cm pie dish (5cm deep). Lightly oil pie dish and line with pastry, allowing a little overhang.

Roll remaining pastry for the top of the pie so it's just larger than the pie dish. Cut small holes in the top of the top pastry, 5mm apart. Place on a baking paper-lined oven tray. Refrigerate pastry base and top until chilled (30 minutes).

Put cubed pear in a bowl and add butter, sugar, cinnamon and lemon juice, tossing well to combine. Transfer to a baking dish that holds them snugly.

Bake in a preheated 180°C (gas mark 4) oven for 20–30 minutes or until pears are softened but still holding their shape. Remove from oven and transfer to a bowl, adding the blueberries while the pears are still warm. Mix well. Allow to cool slightly (20 minutes), then drain through a sieve to remove excess liquid.

Take pastry from refrigerator and spoon fruit mixture into the lined pie dish. Brush the rim of the pastry case with egg wash, then drape remaining pastry over the pie dish. Trim, then press pastry edges firmly together to seal. Crimp the rim using your forefinger and thumb.

Brush the pastry with egg wash, then sprinkle with Demerara sugar.

Bake in a preheated 180°C (gas mark 4) oven for 35–40 minutes or until the pastry is crisp and golden-brown in colour.

Key Lime Pie

This all-American dessert, with its 'yin and yang' combination of sweetened condensed milk and zingy lime and a crunchy, grainy biscuit base, has been given an Asian update with the addition of Blackcurrant and Ginger Compote.

MAKES A 27CM PIE, SERVING 10–12 PEOPLE

CRUST
125g crushed digestive biscuits
3 tbsp granulated sugar
pinch of salt
110g unsalted butter, melted

FILLING
2 × 495g tins sweetened condensed milk
7 egg yolks
240ml fresh lime juice
4 tsp lime zest

BLACKCURRANT AND GINGER COMPOTE
200g frozen blackcurrants
3 balls stem ginger, very finely chopped, and 2 tbsp reserved ginger syrup
100g granulated sugar

Place crushed biscuits in a medium bowl. Mix in sugar and salt, then add melted butter and stir until crumbs are moist. Press mixture onto the bottom and up the sides of a 27cm loose-bottomed tart tin (3cm deep).

Bake in a preheated 180°C (gas mark 4) oven for about 10 minutes or until set and lightly browned. Allow crust to cool completely.

Whisk together condensed milk and egg yolks in a medium bowl. Add lime juice and zest and whisk until blended. Pour filling into cooled crust.

Bake in the preheated oven until filling is set, about 25 minutes. Transfer to a rack and cool to room temperature. Cover and refrigerate pie until chilled (minimum 2 hours or overnight).

To make the compote, place blackcurrants, stem ginger, ginger syrup and sugar in a small heavy-based saucepan and heat gently until the sugar has dissolved and some but not all of the blackcurrants are beginning to release their juices. Remove from heat and refrigerate until cold.

Cut pie into wedges. Spoon Blackcurrant and Ginger Compote on top to serve.

Orange Blossom and White Chocolate Cheesecake Pie with Roast Rhubarb

Strictly speaking, this is not a pie but it's just too good to leave out. The orange blossom adds a lovely flowery scent and the rhubarb adds a big bouncy punch.

MAKES A 22CM PIE, SERVING 8–12 PEOPLE

PASTRY BASE
½ quantity of Basic Sweet Pastry
(see page 193)

CHEESECAKE FILLING
180g white chocolate
900g cream cheese, softened
250g caster sugar
4 eggs
1 tsp vanilla extract
2 tbsp orange blossom water
2 tbsp orange zest

ROAST RHUBARB
500g rhubarb, rinsed and cut into fingers
80g caster sugar

Make a half-quantity of Basic Sweet Pastry ahead and rest it as required. Roll out 300g of the pastry on a lightly floured surface to 5mm thick and line the bottom of a 22cm spring-form cake tin. Prick all over with a fork.

Bake in a preheated 180°C (gas mark 4) oven for 15–20 minutes until lightly brown in colour.

To make the filling, first melt the white chocolate by chopping it into small pieces and placing it in a medium bowl over a double boiler of simmering water. Allow half the chocolate to melt, then remove from the heat. Set aside over warmed water until completely melted. Be careful not to overcook or the chocolate will seize.

Using an electric mixer, beat cream cheese with caster sugar on a low speed until silky and creamed (about 2 minutes). Add eggs one at a time until smooth, making sure you scrape the sides of the bowl as you go. Next add the vanilla, orange blossom water and orange zest. Slowly pour in the melted white chocolate and mix until well combined.

Pour the mixture into the baked pastry case. Wrap aluminium foil around the base and up sides of cake tin to protect it from the water bath. Place cake tin in a large roasting pan with high sides and fill pan with water so it reaches one-third of the way up the outside of the cake tin.

Bake in a preheated 180°C (gas mark 4) oven for 45–50 minutes. The centre will still be slightly wobbly once cooked. Remove cheesecake from oven and allow to cool and set for 4 hours before serving; even better, cool then place in the refrigerator overnight.

When removing the cheese cake from the cake ring/tin, run a small knife around the edge, then carefully lift off the cake ring/tin. You may like to smooth the side using a palette knife dipped in hot water.

To roast rhubarb, preheat oven to 180°C (gas mark 4). Put the rhubarb in a shallow dish or baking tin with sides, tip the sugar over, toss together, then arrange rhubarb in a single layer. Cover with aluminium foil and roast for 15 minutes. Remove foil. The sugar should have dissolved. Give the contents a little shake and roast for another 5 minutes or until tender and juices are syrupy. Test with a sharp knife; the rhubarb should feel tender, not mushy, and have kept its shape.

Serve cheesecake with Roast Rhubarb.

Raspberry Meringue Pie with Coconut Macaroon Pastry

**The raspberry curd and coconut macaroon pastry combination is
exceptional, not only for its flavour and texture, but also for its colour.
I prefer to leave in the raspberry seeds for extra texture.**

MAKES A 23CM PIE, SERVING 10–12 PEOPLE

PASTRY
1 quantity of Coconut Macaroon
Pastry (see page 196)

RASPBERRY CURD
250g raspberries, fresh or frozen
3 tsp cold water
juice and zest of ½ lemon
90g unsalted butter, chopped
200g caster sugar
2 tsp cornflour
2 whole eggs
5 egg yolks

MERINGUE TOPPING
4 egg whites
100g caster sugar

Make the Coconut Macaroon Pastry ahead, wrap in plastic and
rest it overnight in the refrigerator. The next day press pastry into
a 23cm round loose-bottomed tart tin, trimming edges. Refrigerate
for 1 hour.

Bake in a preheated 180°C (gas mark 4) oven for 15–20 minutes or
until edges are lightly coloured. Cool shell on a rack for 5 minutes,
then press the base and sides with the back of a spoon to compact
it. Allow it to cool completely before filling.

To make the curd, place raspberries and water in a small saucepan
over a medium heat then cover and cook for 2 minutes, stirring
a couple of times, until the fruit releases plenty of juice and has
collapsed. Transfer raspberries and juice to a heatproof bowl with
remaining curd ingredients and cook over just-simmering water,
stirring constantly, until mixture thickens (approximately 20
minutes). If you wish, strain Raspberry Curd through a sieve then
pour into the cooled tart shell. Refrigerate to set (approximately
2 hours).

To make Meringue Topping, place egg whites in a clean bowl and
beat using an electric mixer until stiff. Slowly add caster sugar
a little at a time, beating well until a thick meringue is formed.
Dollop meringue over Raspberry Curd to cover completely.

Bake in a preheated 200°C (gas mark 6) oven for 10–15 minutes,
just until tips of meringue are lightly browned. Serve chilled.

Rhubarb, Blueberry and Strawberry Shortcake Pie

Shortcakes are making a comeback. Next time you want to have a treat to take into the office or around to your best friend's house for a cup of tea, make this. It's lovely and homey.

MAKES A 20–22CM PIE, SERVING 8 PEOPLE

SHORTCAKE
125g butter, softened
125g sugar
1 egg
225g standard plain flour
25g cornflour
1 tsp baking powder

FRUIT FILLING
3–4 stalks rhubarb
3 tbsp granulated sugar
100g fresh or frozen strawberries
130g fresh or frozen blueberries

To make shortcake, put the softened butter and sugar in a mixing bowl and beat until light and fluffy, then beat in egg. Sift flour, cornflour and baking powder and beat until just mixed. Scoop two-thirds of the dough into a shallow 20–22cm round cake tin lined with non-stick baking paper. Press the dough evenly over the bottom and up the sides, approximately 3cm high. Set aside the remaining dough for the topping and cover with clingfilm.

To prepare fruit, trim and slice rhubarb and put it in a large non-stick frying pan with sugar. Place over a low heat and shake the pan every now and then, until fruit is almost tender. Trim and slice strawberries and add to pan along with blueberries. Give the pan another shake and set aside until the mixture cools to lukewarm.

Spread warm fruit over shortcake base, then dab pinches of remaining dough over the top, allowing a little of the fruit to peep through.

Bake in a preheated 200°C (gas mark 6) oven for about 30 minutes or until shortcake is a light golden-brown colour. Remove from oven and allow to cool for 10 minutes before turning out onto a cooling rack, and then onto a plate. Serve warm, cool or cold, dusted with icing sugar if liked and with lightly whipped cream on the side.

Nutmeg and Rosemary Custard Tarts

When I was growing up, we used to regularly bake traditional custard tarts, so they bring back lovely memories for me. I would break one on purpose so I could eat it! I have added a sprig of rosemary for a perfume scent – a lovely touch that makes a welcome change from boring old vanilla extract.

MAKES 8 × 10CM INDIVIDUAL TARTS

PASTRY
1 quantity of Basic Short Pastry (see page 197) or Basic Sweet Pastry (see page 193)

NUTMEG AND ROSEMARY CUSTARD
600ml full-fat milk
1 large sprig rosemary
6 egg yolks
75g caster sugar
1 whole nutmeg

TO SERVE
icing sugar, for dusting (optional)
8 tips of rosemary (optional)

Make pastry ahead and rest it as required. On a lightly floured surface, roll out the pastry until slightly larger than the tart tins being used, ensuring pastry is 3–4mm thick. Line the tart tins, ensuring that the pastry is well tucked into the contours and the edges are trimmed. Put these on a baking tray and chill for 30 minutes.

To make custard, put milk and rosemary sprig into a saucepan and heat until lukewarm. Put egg yolks and sugar into a bowl and beat until pale and creamy. Pour warmed milk onto the yolks and stir well – do not whisk or you will get bubbles. Strain into a jug and pour carefully into tart cases. Grate fresh nutmeg liberally over surface of each tart.

Bake in a preheated 200°C (gas mark 6) oven for 10 minutes, then lower heat to 170°C (gas mark 3) and bake until filling is just set and pastry is just starting to turn a golden colour, about another 10 minutes. Don't over-bake as the custard should be a bit wobbly when the tartlets come out of the oven. The egg custard will continue to cook as it cools.

When tartlets are cooled, remove from tins and let cool completely on a rack. Lightly dust with icing sugar around the pastry edges, if desired, and place a small tip of rosemary on top of each. Serve at room temperature.

Oma's Dutch Apple Tart

In Holland, my father's home country, this classic tart is enjoyed with strong coffee in the afternoon. The custard addition makes it very moist. If you don't like sultanas, then just leave them out. Traditionally this is served cold, but it tastes equally great served warm with a good-sized ball of ice cream or, for extra luxury, some caramel sauce.

MAKES A 20–22CM TART, SERVING 8 PEOPLE

PASTRY
1 quantity of Basic Sweet Pastry (see page 193) or Gingerbread Crust Sweet Pastry (see page 195)

CUSTARD
100ml milk, plus 2 tbsp
10g granulated sugar
10g custard powder

FRUIT FILLING
5 medium Granny Smith apples, peeled, cored and sliced, then placed in a bowl of water with the juice of 1 lemon to prevent browning
100g sultanas
100g white sponge or other cake crumbs
½ tbsp lemon juice
2 tsp cinnamon

GLAZE
1 quantity of Apricot Glaze (see page 209)

Make pastry ahead and rest it as required. On a lightly floured surface roll out pastry into a sheet about 4mm thick, and large enough to cover a greased 20–22cm deep loose-bottomed tart tin. Use the rolling pin to pick up pastry and lay it over the tin. Gently press pastry into the tin so that it fills all contours. Be careful not to stretch pastry or it will tear, or shrink back in the oven. Chill in the refrigerator for 30 minutes, or more if the pastry still feels soft. Reserve scraps for the trellis top.

To make custard, place first amount of milk and sugar in a small saucepan. Stir and bring to the boil. Mix the 2 tablespoon of milk with the custard powder in a bowl. Add boiled milk to custard mix, then pour into saucepan and return to a medium heat to thicken. Cool before use.

To make fruit filling, drain and dry apples well before combining with the other filling ingredients. Mix remaining ingredients along with cooled custard in a bowl with the apples. Cover with clingfilm until required – this filling should be kept for no more than 2 days in the refrigerator.

Place prepared apple filling in pastry case, ensuring that it is full to 1cm from the top and well packed down.

On a lightly floured surface, roll out remaining pastry to approximately 3mm thick and at least 25cm long. Cut dough lengthways into 5–10mm-wide strips and lay each strip over the top of the tart to create an attractive lattice effect. Trim off any excess from the edges.

Bake in a preheated 190°C (gas mark 5) oven for 40 minutes or until golden-brown.

Allow to cool for 45 minutes–1 hour before removing from tin. Leave base of the tin in place as this makes the tart easier to handle. Place on a cooling rack. Using a pastry brush, glaze the lattice top with hot Apricot Glaze.

Mini Christmas Deluxe Fruit Mince Tarts

This filling makes more than the 48 mini tarts suggested, so either keep it or use it again later on. If you want to make the filling even better, make it one month before, which will really macerate the fruit in the sherry – you can even add a splash more every week. Rather than make a star or pipe almond cream on, I have kept the full top on and then sprinkled caster sugar over once they come out of the oven. Yum!

MAKES 48 MINI TARTS

FILLING
160g cranberries
160g currants
160g sultanas
200g grated apple
180g suet or butter
150g soft brown sugar
150g mixed peel
100ml sherry
1 tsp salt
2 tsp mixed spice
2 tsp nutmeg
¼ lemon, washed

PASTRY
1 quantity of Basic Sweet Pastry (see page 193) or Gingerbread Crust Sweet Pastry (see page 195)

GLAZE
1 egg beaten with 1 tbsp water, for egg wash (optional)
2 tbsp caster sugar (optional)

Put all filling ingredients through a mincer or finely chop, ensuring that all the ingredients are well combined. Place in a clean airtight container and seal. You can refrigerate it for up to 2 weeks before using.

Make your choice of pastry ahead and rest it as required. On a lightly floured surface, roll out the pastry into a sheet about 3mm thick. Using a 6.5cm round cutter, cut out 24 bases to line two mini muffin trays. Gently press pastry inside the muffin cups to avoid any cracking around the bases.

Using a round or star-shaped cutter, cut 24 tart tops from remaining rolled pastry and set aside. Reserve any pastry scraps. Mould, wrap and place back into the freezer for later use.

Using a teaspoon, fill each pastry-lined case to just below the rim with the filling (approximately 30g each). Lightly brush or spray edges of the pastry cases with water. Place round tops over filling, pressing slightly around edges to seal tops to the bottom, or, if using star-shaped tops, place them in the middle of the filling. If desired, lightly glaze tops with egg wash.

Bake in a preheated 180°C (gas mark 4) oven for 15 minutes or until light golden-brown. Sprinkle with caster sugar, if wished, while tarts are still hot. Allow to cool a little, then remove from trays and store in an airtight container.

Treacle Tart

This seriously sweet and delicious treat from yesteryear will definitely be found in your grandmother's recipe book. Serve warm or at room temperature with clotted cream.

MAKES A 20CM TART, SERVING 6–8 PEOPLE

PASTRY

1 quantity of Basic Short Pastry (see page 197) or Basic Sweet Pastry (see page 193)

FILLING

450g golden syrup
30g unsalted butter, cubed
1 large egg, beaten
3 tbsp double cream
grated zest of 2 lemons
4 heaped tbsp wholemeal breadcrumbs

Make your choice of pastry ahead and rest it as required. Roll out on a lightly floured surface until the pastry is 3mm thick. Carefully line a 20cm tart tin with the pastry and chill for 15–20 minutes. Line the pastry with aluminium foil and fill with baking blind material.

Bake blind (see page 214) in a preheated 190°C (gas mark 5) oven for 15 minutes. Remove foil and weights, return to the oven and turn the heat down to 180°C (gas mark 4). Bake for 5 more minutes.

Place golden syrup into a saucepan and warm very gently over a low heat. Remove from heat, add butter and stir until melted. Make sure the mixture is just warm, not too hot.

Beat together egg and cream in a separate bowl and then add to syrup, with lemon zest and breadcrumbs. Stir to mix evenly, then pour into baked pastry case.

If desired, you can add a lattice top by cutting strips of rolled pastry and arranging them on top.

Bake in a preheated 170°C (gas mark 3) oven for 25–30 minutes until the filling sets to a gel. Remove from the oven and leave for 20–30 minutes before serving warm. Do not serve directly from the oven as the tart will be burning hot.

Apricot, Almond and Fennel Tart

**Apart from the fennel infusion this tart is a French classic. I love
the way the little tips of the apricot become caramelised, almost burnt.
They look great. A dusting of icing sugar around the edges and some
fresh pouring cream finish it nicely. Serve hot or cold.**

MAKES A 20CM TART, SERVING 6 PEOPLE

PASTRY
1 quantity of Butter Puff Pastry
(see page 203)

ALMOND CREAM
50g butter, softened
50g granulated sugar
1 egg
50g ground almonds

**APRICOT AND FENNEL
FILLING**
10 apricots, with the skin on
100g granulated sugar
1 tbsp whole fennel seeds, lightly
bruised

GLAZE
1 quantity of Apricot Glaze (see
page 209), optional

Make pastry the day before and store wrapped in the refrigerator.

To make Almond Cream, place butter and sugar into a mixing
bowl and, using a wooden spoon, cream until light and fluffy.

Slowly add egg and beat until combined, then beat in ground
almonds. Cover and set aside until required.

Wash and dry the apricots. Cut each apricot in half, remove and
discard the stone and cut into quarters. Place in a bowl with
sugar and bruised fennel seeds. Toss to mix thoroughly and coat
apricots. Cover bowl with clingfilm and macerate for 2–4 hours,
tossing every so often to coat apricots again. Reserve any syrup
that forms.

On a floured surface, roll out the pastry to approximately 4mm
thick to fit inside a greased 20cm fluted flan ring or loose-
bottomed tart tin. Trim top edges with a sharp knife.

Fill the pastry case with a thin layer of Almond Cream, then
arrange macerated apricots around the outside, working inwards
until tart is well packed with fruit. Make sure skins are facing down
and the flesh is facing upwards on a slight angle. Pour reserved
fennel syrup evenly over the apricots. Leave tart to rest for
30 minutes.

Bake in a preheated 220°C (gas mark 7) oven for 40–45 minutes or
until fruit topping has turned dark at the edges.

Brush with hot Apricot Glaze while still hot (or leave plain and
sprinkle with icing sugar just before serving).

Hazelnut and Coconut Shortbread with Strawberries and Blueberries

Shortbread has become popular again. This version has a hazelnut and coconut base topped with freshly made vanilla custard and piles of fresh strawberries and blueberries. But don't limit yourself just to berries – the choice of fresh fruits is endless.

MAKES A 20CM TART, SERVING 8 PEOPLE

SHORTBREAD DOUGH
1 large egg
100g standard plain flour
75g butter, softened, cubed
40g caster sugar
25g ground hazelnuts
20g shredded coconut

FILLING
250ml full-fat milk
4 egg yolks
50g granulated sugar
1 tsp vanilla extract, with seeds
30g cornflour
400g fresh strawberries and blueberries
shredded coconut, for decoration

Whisk egg in a cup with a fork and set aside half to use in the Shortbread Dough. Beat the other half with a tablespoon of water for egg wash.

To make dough, mix flour, butter, sugar, half the egg and ground hazelnuts in the food processor until combined. Add shredded coconut then tip dough out onto a floured surface and bring it together with your hands, ensuring coconut is mixed in evenly. Press dough flat, cover with clingfilm and chill for 30 minutes or overnight.

On a lightly floured surface, roll out dough, then place it inside a 20cm round baking tin and brush surface with egg wash.

Bake in a preheated 170°C (gas mark 5) oven for 25–30 minutes or until lightly golden and baked through. Allow to cool, then carefully remove the baked shortbread base from the tin and transfer to a cooling rack. Leave until completely cold.

To make the filling, bring the milk to the boil in a saucepan. In a mixing bowl, beat egg yolks together with sugar, vanilla and cornflour. Pour hot milk over the egg mixture, beating constantly. Return mixture to the saucepan and bring it back to a gentle simmer over a low heat. Cook custard through for 2–3 minutes, stirring to prevent it from burning. You will notice the custard thickening throughout this process. When the correct consistency is reached, remove from heat and allow to cool.

Spread cooled custard mixture evenly over baked shortbread base and arrange fresh berries attractively on top. Sprinkle with shredded coconut.

Fresh Fig and Toasted Hazelnut Spiced Shortbread Tart

Fresh figs can be hard to find out of season so check their availability before you attempt to make this stunning tart. Trust me: they are worth the effort of waiting for and buying. The addition of Chinese five spice brings an aniseed flavour to the shortbread base, but can easily be replaced with mixed spice if you don't like it. Drizzled with runny honey this tart is simply beautiful.

MAKES A 16CM TART, SERVING 4 PEOPLE

SHORTBREAD DOUGH
50g whole blanched hazelnuts
100g standard plain flour
75g butter, softened, in pieces
40g caster sugar
1 tsp Chinese five spice
1 medium egg yolk

TOPPING
150ml double cream
1 tsp vanilla extract
2 tbsp icing sugar, plus extra to dust
6 figs, quartered
approximately 100ml runny honey

Scatter hazelnuts on a baking tray and toast in a preheated 190°C (gas mark 5) oven for 6–7 minutes until golden, then leave to cool (you can now turn the oven off). Grind up half the hazelnuts in a food processor, then roughly chop the rest.

To make the dough, mix flour, butter, sugar, Chinese five spice, egg yolk and ground hazelnuts in the food processor until combined. Tip dough out onto a floured surface and bring it together with your hands. Press dough flat, cover with clingfilm and chill for 30 minutes or overnight.

On a lightly floured surface, roll out dough to a 16cm-diameter circle and transfer it onto a baking paper-lined oven tray.

Bake in a preheated 190°C oven for 20 minutes or until lightly golden. Allow to cool for 5 minutes, then transfer to a cooling rack and leave until completely cold.

Whip cream, vanilla and icing sugar into stiff peaks and then pipe it on the shortcake base almost to the edge. Pile on figs and then sprinkle over chopped hazelnuts. Dust with extra icing sugar and drizzle with honey.

Gingernut Lemon Meringue Pie in a Glass

This has all the elements of a lemon meringue pie . . . a crunchy base (gingernut, in fact), tangy lemon curd and fluffy meringue. Italian meringue is made with a hot sugar syrup, which results in a firmer texture that holds its shape well.

SERVES 4 IN INDIVIDUAL GLASSES

12 Gingernut Biscuits (see page 211 or use shop-bought ones)

LEMON CURD
150g granulated sugar
2 tsp cornflour
juice and zest of 3 medium juicy lemons
5 egg yolks
75g butter

ITALIAN MERINGUE
200g granulated sugar
60ml water
5 egg whites, at room temperature
¼ tsp cream of tartar

Make biscuits in advance and store in an airtight container to ensure they remain crisp.

Prepare curd a day ahead. In a bowl, combine sugar, cornflour, lemon juice, lemon zest and egg yolks. Stir together with a hand whisk, but don't whip any air into the mixture. Set over a saucepan of simmering water and gently whisk until mixture thickens; halfway through add butter and continue to whisk. This will take approximately 5 minutes. Take care not to allow mixture to get too hot or eggs will scramble. Once curd has thickened, cover with clingfilm and refrigerate.

To make the Italian Meringue, in a small saucepan combine sugar and water over low heat. Swirl the saucepan to dissolve the sugar completely. Do not stir. Increase heat and boil to soft ball stage (115°C). Use a sugar thermometer for accuracy. Brush down inside wall of saucepan with a wet pastry brush. This will help prevent sugar crystals from forming around the sides and falling in and causing a chain reaction.

In the bowl of an electric mixer, whip eggs whites on low speed until foamy. Add cream of tartar. Increase speed to medium, and beat until soft peaks form.

With mixer running, pour hot sugar syrup in a thin stream over fluffed egg whites. Beat until egg white mixture is stiff and glossy. Place in a piping bag and prepare to use immediately.

To assemble, break the Gingernut Biscuits into small pieces and set aside. Transfer curd to a piping bag, then create alternating layers of curd, biscuit pieces and meringue into four glasses, finishing with a layer of Italian Meringue. Level with a palette knife and decorate with pieces of biscuit and a dusting of icing sugar.

Linzer Torte with Spiced Melting Moment Topping

This classic Austrian torte is famous worldwide for its delicate almond-based pastry fragrantly spiced with cinnamon and cloves, and jam filling that provides a light, fruity richness. Ensure you use a high-quality jam, abundant with fruit. I've added a melting moment piped biscuit topping; pure genius! Serve chilled with rich cream or vanilla ice cream.

MAKES A 33CM × 9CM TART, SERVING 6–8 PEOPLE

PASTRY
½ quantity of Linzer Pastry (see page 194)

FILLING
400g good-quality raspberry, blackcurrant or redcurrant jam

TOPPING
30g flaked almonds
40g icing sugar
125g butter, softened
2 drops vanilla extract
125g standard plain flour
15g cornflour
1 tsp ground cinnamon

Make Linzer Pastry ahead and rest it as required. On a lightly floured surface, roll out pastry to 3–4mm thick. Carefully roll it up on the rolling pin and unroll it into a 33cm × 9cm tart tin. Take care as the pastry will be rather soft. Carefully press pastry into the corners of the tart tin and patch any holes. Trim edges using a sharp knife to ensure they are smooth and even.

Stir jam until it is lump-free and spread evenly into the pastry base.

Crumble some flaked almonds between your fingertips until you have smaller pieces to sprinkle around the edge of the tart, then set aside.

To make topping, place icing sugar, butter and vanilla extract into a mixing bowl. Using an electric beater, beat until the mixture is very soft and fluffy. It is important that the mixture is well creamed and soft, otherwise it will be hard to pipe.

Sift flour, cornflour and cinnamon together and add to creamed mixture. Beat together until dry ingredients are well mixed, but do not over-mix. Place mixture into a piping bag fitted with a small star tube, and pipe over the jam filling diagonally one way then the other to create a trellis pattern. Sprinkle crushed almond flakes around the edge of the tart.

Pipe small shapes of leftover mixture onto a baking paper-lined oven tray and bake in a preheated 170°C (gas mark 3) oven for 10–12 minutes to make petit four biscuits to serve with coffee or tea.

Bake tart in a preheated 180°C (gas mark 4) oven for 30–35 minutes or until golden-brown in colour. Take care as the base pastry will bake fast due to the high amount of butter and oil (from the almonds).

Peach, Rhubarb and Vanilla Tart

**Serve this delicious tart as an afternoon treat with a cup of tea.
There will be extra jam so place into a sterilised jar and keep in the
refrigerator to have on toast.**

MAKES A 23CM TART, SERVING 12 PEOPLE

**PEACH, RHUBARB AND
VANILLA JAM**
5 stalks rhubarb, diced
60ml lemon juice
1 vanilla pod, seeds scraped out
6 peaches (equals 3 cups
mashed)
250g granulated sugar
2 tsp dry pectin

BASE
185g butter, softened
250g caster sugar
1 tsp vanilla extract
3 egg yolks
400g standard plain flour
3 tsp baking powder

TOPPING
5 egg whites
100g caster sugar
140g shredded coconut
2 tsp vanilla extract

Make jam ahead. Place rhubarb in a pan over medium heat with
lemon juice and vanilla seeds. Cook rhubarb until soft, 5–10
minutes. Remove peach skins, then pit and cut peaches into bite-
sized pieces. Mash peaches and place into pan with rhubarb. Stir
over medium-high heat and let mixture come to a boil. Reduce
heat and cook for 30 minutes.

In a separate bowl, mix together sugar and pectin. Add sugar and
pectin mixture to pan containing peach and rhubarb. Stir together
and bring to a boil. Pour into a sterilised jar to set.

To make the tart, preheat oven to 150°C (gas mark 2). Lightly
grease a 23cm round tart tin. In a mixing bowl, cream together
butter and sugar until light and fluffy, then add vanilla extract.
Add egg yolks, one at a time, beating well after each addition.

Sift flour and baking powder together and fold through creamed
mixture. The dough will seem quite crumbly, this is normal. Press
dough into the base and up the sides of the lined cake tin.

Prepare coconut meringue topping. In a clean bowl, use an electric
mixer to beat egg whites until they form soft peaks. Gradually add
caster sugar a tablespoon at a time, while beating until egg whites
form stiff, glossy peaks. Use a spatula to gently fold in the coconut
and vanilla extract.

Using a spatula, spread a generous layer of jam over the dough.
Spoon and spread coconut meringue over jam. Make sure all the
jam is covered with meringue.

Bake in the preheated oven for 20–25 minutes or until the
meringue top is a soft pink eggshell colour (it is normal for the
meringue to crack). Remove from the oven and cool in the tin
for 20 minutes. Carefully remove from tart tin and place on a
cooling rack.

Once cool, cut into wedges. The tart can be kept in an airtight
container for up to one week.

Walnut and Manuka Honey Tart with Orange Greek Yoghurt

This tart contains all the gooey and nutty essential elements of a great dessert. The orange-infused yoghurt is a wonderful citrus counterpoint to all the sweetness. It's so good you will want more!

MAKES A 35CM × 10CM TART, SERVING 8 PEOPLE

PASTRY
1 quantity of Basic Sweet Pastry (see page 193)

ORANGE GREEK YOGHURT
500g plain unsweetened Greek yoghurt
zest and juice of 1 orange
2 tbsp icing sugar

FILLING
120g butter
120g manuka honey
140g brown sugar
100ml double cream
200g walnuts, roughly chopped

Make pastry ahead and rest it as required. Roll out 300g of the pastry (freeze the rest wrapped in clingfilm for future use) on a lightly floured surface to 3mm thick and use it to line a 35cm × 10cm loose-bottomed tart tin. Trim the pastry edges, then refrigerate for 1 hour.

Line tart with aluminium foil and fill with baking blind material. Bake blind (see page 214) in a preheated 180°C (gas mark 4) oven for 10 minutes. Remove foil and weights and bake until dry and crisp (10 minutes).

Mix together the Orange Greek Yoghurt ingredients and refrigerate until needed.

To make the filling, melt butter in a saucepan over a low-medium heat until the butter melts. Add honey, sugar and cream. Stir until boiling, then allow to boil for a further 2 minutes without stirring. Remove pan from heat and stir in chopped walnuts. Pour mixture into cooked pastry case.

Bake in a preheated 190°C (gas mark 5) oven for 15 minutes until bubbling and golden.

Allow to cool, then cut into slabs with a hot knife and serve with Orange Greek Yoghurt.

Baklava 'Pie' with Elderflower Yoghurt

A Baklava Pie – why not? Baking this in a pie tin makes sense and the peach makes a welcome sweet fruit influence rather than the standard nutty version. Serve as a dessert together with a dollop of Elderflower yoghurt.

MAKES A 22CM PIE, SERVING 12 PEOPLE

HONEY AND ORANGE SYRUP

300g granulated sugar
140g runny honey
150ml cold water
2 cinnamon sticks
2 tbsp fresh lemon juice
2 tbsp orange zest

ELDERFLOWER YOGHURT

500g Greek yoghurt
3 tbsp Elderflower cordial

BAKLAVA

200g raw walnuts
260g raw unsalted pistachios, shelled
150g Demerara sugar
2 tsp lemon zest
2 tsp orange zest
1½ tsp ground cinnamon
200g finely chopped dried peaches
20 sheets fresh or thawed filo pastry
150g unsalted butter, melted

Combine all the syrup ingredients in a heavy-based medium saucepan. Bring to the boil over a medium-high heat, stirring until sugar dissolves. Reduce heat to medium and boil until syrup is reduced to 1½ cups (approximately 15 minutes). Transfer to a bowl and cool completely (approximately 2 hours). Syrup can be made the day before.

To make the yoghurt, combine ingredients and refrigerate until needed.

To make baklava, spread walnuts and pistachios on a large roasting tray lined with baking paper. Roast nuts in a preheated 180°C (gas mark 4) oven for 5 minutes. Transfer nuts to a food processor. Add sugar, lemon and orange zests and cinnamon. Process until nuts are ground to medium-fine texture. Transfer mixture to a large bowl and mix in dried peaches.

Place filo sheet stack on the work surface and cover with clingfilm to prevent it drying out. Divide nut mixture into five portions.

Brush a 22cm round loose-bottomed cake tin with melted butter. Take two sheets of pastry and brush with melted butter, fold in half and use to line the base of your tin. Brush pastry with melted butter again, then take another two sheets, brush with butter, fold in half and place on the first layer. Top with one portion of the nut mixture. Repeat process four times until top sheet is almost level with the top of the cake tin. This top layer won't require brushing with butter.

Using a sharp knife, cut the filo layers into 12 wedges (try to avoid cutting through to the bottom of the cake tin).

Bake in a preheated 190°C (gas mark 5) oven for 45–50 minutes or until golden.

Slowly spoon cold Honey and Orange Syrup over hot Baklava. Let stand 2–3 hours or until it cools to room temperature.

Basic Recipes

Sweet and Short Pastry

The main difference between sweet and short pastry is the amount of sugar used. There are four methods of making sweet and short pastry, but the two most common methods involve creaming and blending.

Creaming Method

1. Beat butter, salt and sugar until light, creamy and fluffy.

2. Continue beating on low speed while adding liquid or egg.

3. Slowly mix in dry ingredients and mix until a clear, smooth paste is formed. Do not over-mix.

4. The pastry is ready for processing.

Blending Method

1. Mix butter and flour together until no lumps are left and mix resembles ground almonds or a crumble.

2. Mix liquid or eggs with sugar and salt, then slowly add to the dry mixture while mixing on a slow speed.

3. Mix until a clear, smooth paste is formed. Do not over-mix.

4. The pastry is ready for processing.

Creating Shortness in Sweet and Short Pastry

The mixing methods used in making sweet and short pastry are designed to coat the flour particles with fat, thus protecting the development of the protein (gluten) network when the liquids are added. Mixing this way will always ensure that a short, tender pastry is obtained, provided it has been mixed for the correct length of time.

Points to Consider when Processing Sweet and Short Pastry

- Do not over-mix the dough as this will toughen the gluten strands, causing toughness and shrinkage in the pastry.

- Avoid excessive handling of the pastry as your hands will warm it up too much and make it too soft to work.

- Work in a cool environment to prevent the dough becoming too soft to handle.

Storage of Sweet and Short Pastry

Unbaked sweet and short pastry can be stored in the refrigerator or freezer, unfilled or filled. It is advisable to thaw sweet or short pastry in the refrigerator overnight, then let it stand at room temperature for approximately 30 minutes before using.

Faults in Sweet and Short Pastry

FAULTS / CAUSES	NOT ENOUGH FAT, EGG, SUGAR	TOO STRONG FLOUR USED	TOO LITTLE EGG/LIQUID USED	TOO MUCH EGG/LIQUID USED	NOT RESTED BEFORE BAKING	TOO MUCH AERATION	TOO MUCH SUGAR	OVEN TEMP TOO HIGH	OVEN TEMP TOO LOW	TOO MUCH FAT USED	OVER-MIXED	UNDER-MIXED	TOO MUCH FILLING
Tough pastry	•	•	•	•							•		
Shrinkage	•	•		•	•						•		
Distorted shape	•	•		•	•						•		
Dense texture	•	•	•								•		
Dark in colour							•	•					
Lack of colour	•								•				
Pastry breaking, too short						•	•			•		•	
Brown spot on the crust							•						
Filling spilling out during baking													•

Baking Guidelines

This chart is a general guide to baking sweet and short pastry. All times and temperatures are guides only and will vary from oven to oven.

PRODUCT	TEMPERATURE	TIME (VARIABLE)
Unfilled sweet pastry	180–190°C (gas mark 4–5)	18–20 minutes
Filled sweet pastry	180–190°C (gas mark 4–5)	20–25 minutes
Unfilled short pastry	200–220°C (gas mark 6–7)	18–20 minutes
Filled short pastry	215–220°C (gas mark 7)	20–25 minutes
Reheating sweet and short pastry products	180–190°C (gas mark 4–5)	15–25 minutes

Cooling

Baked sweet or short pastry should be cooled on a cooling rack to prevent sweating. Pies should be allowed to cool slightly before being removed from their tins, which will stop the pie collapsing and becoming soggy on the bottom.

Basic Sweet Pastry

170g butter, softened
85g caster sugar
1 small egg
4 drops vanilla extract
zest of ½ lemon
260g standard plain flour

In a large mixing bowl, lightly beat butter and sugar with a wooden spoon until a light creamy consistency has been achieved. Add egg, vanilla and lemon zest and mix until combined. Add flour and mix to a paste just until paste comes clean off the bowl. Be careful not to over-mix or the pastry will become too elastic and doughy. Cover with clingfilm and refrigerate for 30 minutes or, even better, overnight.

Before using, gently re-work pastry, taking care to ensure it remains cold and firm.

On a lightly floured surface, roll out pastry into a sheet about 3mm thick or as stated in your recipe.

Chocolate Sweet Pastry

170g butter, softened
85g caster sugar
1 medium egg
260g standard plain flour
30g good-quality cocoa powder

In a large mixing bowl, lightly beat butter and sugar with a wooden spoon until a light, creamy consistency has been achieved. Add egg and mix until combined. Sift in flour and cocoa and mix to a paste. Only mix until the paste comes clean off the bowl. Be careful not to over-mix or pastry will become too elastic and doughy. Cover with clingfilm and refrigerate for 30 minutes or, even better, overnight.

Gently re-work pastry before using, taking care to ensure it remains cold and firm.

On a lightly floured surface, roll out pastry into a sheet about 3mm thick or as stated in your recipe.

Linzer Pastry (Spiced Sweet Pastry)

200g standard plain flour
½ tsp ground cloves
1 tsp ground cinnamon
75g ground almonds
100g caster sugar
zest of 1 lemon
225g butter, softened
2 egg yolks
½ tsp vanilla extract

Sift flour, cloves and cinnamon together in a mixing bowl. Add almonds, sugar and lemon zest. In a large bowl, mix together butter, egg yolks and vanilla using a wooden spoon and then add dry ingredients. Continue mixing until well combined and a mass is formed. Shape into a ball, flatten and cover with clingfilm. Place in refrigerator for approximately 1 hour or overnight.

Gingerbread Crust Sweet Pastry

170g butter, softened
85g brown sugar
1 small egg
250g standard plain flour
20g gingerbread spice mixture (see page 210)

In a large mixing bowl, lightly beat butter and brown sugar with a wooden spoon until a light, creamy consistency has been achieved. Add egg and mix until combined. Sift flour and gingerbread spice into the creamed mixture and mix to a paste. Only mix until paste comes clean off the bowl. Be careful not to over-mix or pastry will become too elastic and doughy.

Cover with clingfilm and refrigerate for 30 minutes or, even better, overnight.

Gently re-work pastry before using, taking care to ensure it remains cold and firm.

Soured Cream and Lemon Pastry

150g butter, chilled
190g plain flour
zest of 2 lemons
90ml soured cream

Chop butter into small cubes and then place with flour and lemon zest in a food processor. Blend until it resembles large breadcrumbs. Add soured cream gradually. Check the consistency before adding all of the soured cream and do not add it all if it is not needed.

Turn pastry onto a floured surface and pull together with your hands into a rectangle. Be careful not to over-mix or pastry will become too elastic and doughy.

Cover with clingfilm and refrigerate for 30 minutes or, even better, overnight.

Gently re-work pastry before using, taking care to ensure it remains cold and firm.

Dutch Yeasted Sweet Pastry

FERMENT
75g water
5g active dried yeast
75g standard plain flour
1½ tsp caster sugar

DOUGH
150g standard plain flour
¼ tsp salt
1 small egg
1½ tsp caster sugar
90g butter, softened

For the ferment, place water and yeast in a bowl and whisk to dissolve yeast. Add flour and sugar and stir vigorously for 2 minutes to make a paste. Cover with clingfilm and set aside for 20 minutes to ferment.

To make the dough, mix flour, salt, egg, sugar, butter and yeast ferment together until it forms a mass and dough is well combined and smooth. Don't over-mix dough as this will cause shrinkage during rolling out and baking.

Roll out and set aside on a floured surface for 10 minutes to rest, covered with clingfilm. If you don't use pastry within 10 minutes, refrigerate it to prevent it rising too much.

On a lightly floured surface, roll out pastry into a sheet about 3mm thick or as stated in your recipe.

Coconut Macaroon Pastry

200g desiccated coconut
150g caster sugar
70g standard plain flour
2 eggs, lightly beaten

In a large mixing bowl, combine coconut, sugar and flour. Add eggs and mix well. Press into the base and sides of baking tin with dampened fingers.

Basic Short Pastry (also called Brisée Pastry)

160g standard plain flour
120g butter
good pinch of salt
50ml cold water

Place flour, butter and salt in a large mixing bowl. Using your fingertips, gently rub ingredients together until they resemble rough breadcrumbs. Do not over-mix otherwise butter will begin to melt from the heat of your fingers.

Add water and mix until a dough is formed. Cover with clingfilm and refrigerate for 30 minutes or overnight.

Gently re-work pastry before using, taking care to ensure it remains cold and firm.

On a lightly floured surface, roll out pastry into a sheet about 3mm thick or as stated in your recipe.

Whole-wheat Pastry

80g standard plain flour
80g wholemeal or whole-wheat flour
120g butter
good pinch of salt
70ml cold water

Place the two flours, butter and salt in a large mixing bowl. Using your fingertips, gently rub ingredients together until they resemble rough breadcrumbs. Do not over-mix otherwise butter will begin to melt from the heat of your fingers.

Add water and mix until a dough is formed. Cover with clingfilm and refrigerate for 30 minutes or overnight.

Gently re-work pastry before using, taking care to ensure it remains cold and firm.

On a lightly floured surface, roll out pastry into a sheet about 3mm thick or as stated in your recipe.

Black Sesame Seed Short Pastry

160g standard plain flour
2 tbsp black sesame seeds
120g butter
good pinch of salt
50ml cold water

Place flour, black sesame seeds, butter and salt into a large mixing bowl. Using your fingertips, gently rub ingredients together until they resemble rough breadcrumbs. Do not over-mix otherwise butter will begin to melt from the heat of your fingers.

Add water and mix until a dough is formed. Cover with clingfilm and refrigerate for 30 minutes or overnight.

Gently re-work pastry before using, taking care to ensure it remains cold and firm.

On a lightly floured surface, roll out pastry as stated in your recipe.

Toasted Walnut Short Pastry

50g walnuts, shelled
160g standard plain flour
1 tbsp caster sugar
120g butter
good pinch of salt
50ml cold water

Preheat oven to 170°C (gas mark 3).

Place walnuts on an oven tray and lightly toast in preheated oven until light amber in colour. Finely chop walnuts (1–2mm in size) and set aside.

Place flour, sugar, toasted walnuts, butter and salt into a large mixing bowl. Using your fingertips, gently rub ingredients together until they resemble rough breadcrumbs. Do not over-mix otherwise butter will begin to melt from the heat of your fingers.

Add water and mix until a dough is formed. Cover with clingfilm and refrigerate for 30 minutes or overnight.

Gently re-work pastry before using, taking care to ensure it remains cold and firm.

On a lightly floured surface, roll out pastry as stated in your recipe.

Chilli Polenta Pie Crust

250g standard plain flour
50g coarse polenta
225g butter, cold and 1cm diced
1 tbsp red chilli, deseeded and chopped
as finely as you can
good pinch of salt
1 tbsp cold water

Place flour, polenta, butter, chilli and salt into a large mixing bowl. Using your fingertips, gently rub ingredients together until they resemble rough breadcrumbs. Do not over-mix otherwise butter will begin to melt from the heat of your fingers.

Add water and mix until a dough is formed. Cover with clingfilm and refrigerate for 30 minutes or overnight.

Gently re-work pastry before using, taking care to ensure it remains cold and firm.

On a lightly floured surface, roll out pastry as stated in your recipe.

Fennel Pastry

2 tbsp fennel seeds
160g standard plain flour
120g butter
good pinch of salt
50ml cold water

Place fennel seeds in a pestle and mortar and grind to a rough powder, ensuring that it's not too fine. Set aside.

Place flour, fennel seeds, butter and salt into a large mixing bowl. Using your fingertips, gently rub ingredients together until they resemble rough breadcrumbs. Do not over-mix otherwise butter will begin to melt from the heat of your fingers.

Add water and mix until a dough is formed. Cover with clingfilm and refrigerate for 30 minutes or overnight.

Gently re-work pastry before using, taking care to ensure it remains cold and firm.

On a lightly floured surface, roll out pastry as stated in your recipe.

Toasted Sesame Seed Pastry

2 tbsp sesame seeds
160g standard plain flour
120g butter
good pinch of salt
50ml cold water

Lightly toast sesame seeds in a frying pan over a low heat until amber in colour (this will not take long). Stir and shake pan often to prevent seeds burning. Allow to cool.

Place flour, sesame seeds, butter and salt into a large mixing bowl. Using your fingertips, gently rub ingredients together until they resemble rough breadcrumbs. Do not over-mix otherwise butter will begin to melt from the heat of your fingers.

Add water and mix until a dough is formed. Cover with clingfilm and refrigerate for 30 minutes or overnight.

Gently re-work pastry before using, taking care to ensure it remains cold and firm.

On a lightly floured surface, roll out pastry as stated in your recipe.

Hot Water Pastry for Pork Pies

225g lard
250ml water
500g standard plain flour, plus extra for dusting
1 tsp salt

Place lard and water in a small saucepan and bring to the boil.

Sift flour and salt into a large bowl. Make a well in the flour and pour in warm lard mixture. Mix well to combine, until mixture comes together to form a dough.

Knead for a few minutes, then form into four 125g balls and four 30g balls. Cover with clingfilm and set aside in the refrigerator overnight.

Puff Pastry

Once the initial dough has been formed by mixing together the flour, chilled water, salt and butter to achieve a three-quarter developed dough, there are three methods of incorporating the butter (layering fat). They are known as the Scotch Method (also known as the blitz, rough puff or all-in method), English Method and French Method. For the recipes in this book, I have used the French Method for making puff pastry.

Points to Consider When Making Puff Pastry

- When making puff pastry, ensure that all ingredients are kept cool.
- Always ensure that the dough and layering fat are of the same consistency when incorporating the layering fat.
- Always use chilled water. In summer use iced chilled water (but do not put the ice cubes in the dough as they will not dissolve during mixing).
- Always keep the bench lightly floured during the rolling out process. Never allow the pastry to stick to the bench.
- When rolling and folding the puff pastry use as little dusting flour as possible, and brush away any excess flour before completing each fold.
- When rolling out for each fold, ensure that the open ends are folded back into the centre of the dough.
- Always follow the resting times stated in the recipe to prevent shrinkage in the finished baked product.
- During resting periods keep the pastry covered with clingfilm and keep cool in the refrigerator.
- Always rest the puff pastry products before baking, the longer the better (anywhere from 2–12 hours in the refrigerator). If chilled, allow pastry to return to room temperature before baking.

How Does Puff Pastry Rise?

Once the hundreds of layers of dough and layering fat enter the oven (the oven must be at the correct temperature), the fat melts and the moisture within the dough begins to produce steam. The protein (gluten) in the dough layers begins to expand and separate. The steam pushes the dough layers upwards.

Once the puff pastry has reached its maximum volume and all the moisture within the dough has escaped, the protein (gluten) begins to coagulate (set), giving the pastry its structure. If the puff pastry is taken out of the oven before complete coagulation is achieved, the structure will collapse.

Storage of Puff Pastry

Unbaked puff pastry can be stored in the refrigerator or in the freezer in block or rolled form. Thaw puff pastry in the refrigerator overnight, then let it stand at room temperature for approximately 30 minutes.

Above and left: Steps in making Butter Puff Pastry dough and enclosing the butter, ready for layering.

Butter Puff Pastry (using the French Method)

300g strong bread flour
50g chilled butter
good pinch of salt
150ml ice-cold water (place in the refrigerator overnight)
1 tsp fresh lemon juice
225g chilled butter, for layering

Place flour, first measure of butter and salt into a large mixing bowl. Using your fingers, roughly break up butter into flour. Add ice-cold water and lemon juice, then, using your hands, mix the ingredients to form a firm dough. Tip dough out onto a lightly floured surface and knead for 2–3 minutes. Form into a ball. Cover dough with clingfilm and allow to rest for 5–10 minutes. On a lightly floured surface, use a rolling pin to roll out the dough to a 25cm square approximately 1cm thick.

Ensure layering butter is the same consistency as dough – this can be done by hitting chilled butter with a rolling pin to achieve a 17cm square (the hitting will be enough to soften the butter). Then place butter inside rolled out square of dough.

Fold each corner of dough into the centre to encase layering butter in an envelope, obtaining two layers of dough and one layer of butter (see photographs opposite).

Now give the pastry six 'single turns' as described next (see also photographs on page 204).

Single Turn

1. Roll out the pastry to form a rectangle 1cm thick. Divide the rectangle into thirds.

2. Fold A to C and then D to B to form three layers of pastry.

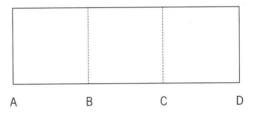

3. Rest the pastry in the refrigerator for 15–20 minutes, covered with a plastic bag to prevent the pastry drying out and forming a skin.

4. Repeat steps 1–3 five times. Make sure the pastry is rested in the refrigerator for 15–20 minutes between each step, covered with a plastic bag to prevent it drying out and forming a skin.

5. You should now have given your pastry six 'single turns'. The pastry is either ready to be rolled out to the final thickness required for your product or it can be kept in the refrigerator for up to three days or in the freezer until required.

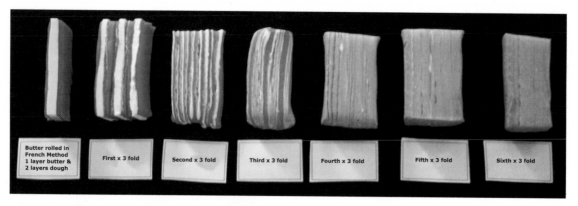

| Butter rolled in French Method 1 layer butter & 2 layers dough | First x 3 fold | Second x 3 fold | Third x 3 fold | Fourth x 3 fold | Fifth x 3 fold | Sixth x 3 fold |

Baking guidelines

The chart below is a general guide to baking puff pastry. All times and temperatures are guides only and will vary from oven to oven.

PRODUCT	TEMPERATURE	TIME (VARIABLE)
Unfilled puff pastry	220–230°C (gas mark 7–8)	18–20 minutes
Filled puff pastry (sweet)	215–220°C (gas mark 7)	20–25 minutes
Filled puff pastry (savoury)	220–225°C (gas mark 7)	25–30 minutes
Reheating puff pastry products	190–200°C (gas mark 5–6)	15–25 minutes

Cooling

Puff pastry should be cooled on a cooling rack to prevent it sweating. Pies should be allowed to cool slightly before being removed from their tins. This will stop the pastry from collapsing.

Top: Shows the layering of the dough (dyed pink to better differentiate the layers) and butter from the first layer through to the sixth 'single turn'.

Above: Folding the pastry to create a 'single turn'.

Faults in Puff Pastry

FAULTS / CAUSES	INCORRECT ROLLING TECHNIQUE	FAT TOO HARD	TOO SHORT REST BEFORE BAKING	UNEVEN OVEN HEAT	TOO MANY TURNS/FOLDS	ROLLED OUT TOO THIN	FLOUR TOO WEAK	LAYERING FAT TOO SOFT	ROOM TEMP TOO WARM	TOO MUCH FAT USED	NOT ENOUGH FAT USED	OVEN TEMP TOO LOW	INCORRECT CUTTING OUT	TOUGH LAYERING FAT USED	FLOUR TOO STRONG	DOUGH MADE TOO FIRM	DOUGH MADE TOO SOFT	SKINNING OF PASTRY	POOR SEALING	INSUFFICIENT TURNS/FOLDS	PASTRY LEFT UNCOVERED
Uneven lift	•	•	•	•									•					•	•	•	
Poor volume	•				•	•	•	•	•	•	•		•				•	•	•		
Distorted shape	•		•	•									•					•		•	
Shrinkage			•												•	•	•				
Fat seepage during baking		•						•		•		•								•	
Tough eating					•						•			•	•	•	•	•			
Filling spilling out			•										•					•			
Skinning																					•

Flavoured Puff Pastry Recipes. From left: Rolling out Olive Butter Puff Pastry; folding Spinach Puff Pastry; sheets of Olive, Spinach and Smoked Paprika butter puff pastries.

Spinach Puff Pastry

50g clean spinach leaves
130ml ice-cold water (place in the refrigerator overnight)
300g strong bread flour
50g chilled butter
good pinch of salt
½ tsp fresh lemon juice
225g chilled butter, for layering

Place spinach in ice-cold water. Using a hand blender, blitz until water is a green colour and leaves are blended through but not puréed, as you want to have flecks of spinach throughout the dough. Set aside.

Place flour, first measure of butter and salt into a large mixing bowl and, using your fingers, roughly break up the butter into the flour. Add ice-cold spinach water and lemon juice. Using your hands, mix ingredients to form a firm dough. Tip the dough out onto a lightly floured surface and knead for 2–3 minutes. Form into a ball. Cover dough with clingfilm and allow to rest for 5–10 minutes. On a lightly floured surface, use a rolling pin to roll out dough to a 25cm square approximately 1cm thick.

Ensure layering butter is the same consistency as the dough – this can be done by hitting the chilled butter with a rolling pin to achieve a 17cm square (the hitting will be enough to soften the butter). Place it inside the rolled out square of dough.

Fold each corner of dough into the centre to encase layering butter in an envelope, creating two layers of dough and one layer of butter.

Now give pastry six 'single turns' as described in the Basic Puff Pastry recipe (see page 203) and cover with clingfilm. Store in refrigerator or freezer until needed.

Smoked Paprika and Black Sesame Seed Puff Pastry

300g strong bread flour
50g chilled butter
good pinch of salt
15g smoked paprika powder
1 tbsp black sesame seeds
150ml ice-cold water (place in the refrigerator overnight)
½ tsp fresh lemon juice
225g chilled butter, for layering

Place flour, first measure of butter, salt, smoked paprika and sesame seeds into a large mixing bowl and, using your fingers, roughly break up the butter into the flour. Add ice-cold water and lemon juice. Using your hands, mix ingredients to form a firm dough. Tip dough out onto a lightly floured surface and knead for 2–3 minutes. Form into a ball. Cover dough with clingfilm and allow to rest for 5–10 minutes. On a lightly floured surface, use a rolling pin to roll out dough to a 25cm square approximately 1cm thick.

Ensure layering butter is the same consistency as the dough – this can be done by hitting the chilled butter with a rolling pin to achieve a 17cm square (the hitting will be enough to soften the butter). Place it inside the rolled out square of dough.

Fold each corner of dough into the centre to encase layering butter in an envelope, creating two layers of dough and one layer of butter.

Now give pastry six 'single turns' as described in the Butter Puff Pastry recipe (see page 203) and cover with clingfilm. Store in refrigerator or freezer until needed.

Olive Butter Puff Pastry

300g strong bread flour
50g chilled butter
good pinch of salt
50g pitted black olives, finely sliced
130ml ice-cold water (place in the refrigerator overnight)
½ tsp fresh lemon juice
225g chilled butter, for layering

Place flour, first measure of butter, salt and olives into a large mixing bowl and, using your fingers, roughly break up the butter into the flour. Add ice-cold water and lemon juice. Using your hands, mix ingredients to form a firm dough. Tip dough out onto a lightly floured surface and knead for 2–3 minutes. Form into a ball. Cover dough with clingfilm and allow to rest for 5–10 minutes. On a lightly floured surface, use a rolling pin to roll out dough to a 25cm square approximately 1cm thick.

Ensure layering butter is the same consistency as the dough – this can be done by hitting the chilled butter with a rolling pin to achieve a 17cm square (the hitting will be enough to soften the butter). Place it inside the rolled out square of dough.

Fold each corner of dough into the centre to encase layering butter in an envelope, creating two layers of dough and one layer of butter.

Now give pastry six 'single turns' as described in the Butter Puff Pastry recipe (see page 203) and cover with clingfilm. Store in refrigerator or freezer until needed.

Curry and Black Kalonji Seed Puff Pastry

300g strong bread flour
50g chilled butter
good pinch of salt
10g curry powder
1½ tbsp black kalonji seeds (black onion seeds)
150ml ice-cold water (place in the refrigerator overnight)
½ tsp fresh lemon juice
225g chilled butter, for layering

Place flour, first measure of butter, salt, curry powder and seeds into a large mixing bowl and, using your fingers, roughly break up the butter into the flour. Add ice-cold water and lemon juice. Using your hands, mix ingredients to form a firm dough. Tip dough out onto a lightly floured surface and knead for 2–3 minutes. Form into a ball. Cover dough with clingfilm and allow to rest for 5–10 minutes. On a lightly floured surface, use a rolling pin to roll out dough to a 25cm square approximately 1cm thick.

Ensure layering butter is the same consistency as the dough – this can be done by hitting the chilled butter with a rolling pin to achieve a 17cm square (the hitting will be enough to soften the butter). Place it inside the rolled out square of dough.

Fold each corner of dough into the centre to encase layering butter in an envelope, creating two layers of dough and one layer of butter.

Now give pastry six 'single turns' as described in the Butter Puff Pastry recipe (see page 203) and cover with clingfilm. Store in refrigerator or freezer until needed.

Chilli and Polenta Puff Pastry

300g strong bread flour
45g coarsely ground polenta
50g chilled butter
good pinch of salt
15g red chilli, deseeded and finely chopped
150ml ice-cold water (place in the refrigerator overnight)
½ tsp fresh lemon juice
225g chilled butter, for layering

Place flour, polenta, first measure of butter, salt and chilli into a large mixing bowl and, using your fingers, roughly break up the butter into the flour. Add ice-cold water and lemon juice. Using your hands, mix ingredients to form a firm dough. Tip dough out onto a lightly floured surface and knead for 2–3 minutes. Form into a ball. Cover dough with clingfilm and allow to rest for 5–10 minutes. On a lightly floured surface, use a rolling pin to roll the dough to a 25cm square approximately 1cm thick.

Ensure layering butter is the same consistency as the dough – this can be done by hitting the chilled butter with a rolling pin to achieve a 17cm square (the hitting will be enough to soften the butter). Place it inside the rolled out square of dough.

Fold each corner of dough into the centre to encase layering butter in an envelope, obtaining two layers of dough and one layer of butter.

Now give pastry six 'single turns' as described in the Butter Puff Pastry recipe (see page 203) and cover with clingfilm. Store in refrigerator or freezer until needed.

Gingerbread Puff Pastry

300g strong bread flour
50g chilled butter
good pinch of salt
25g Gingerbread Spice Mixture (see page 210)
150ml ice-cold water (place in the refrigerator overnight)
½ tsp fresh lemon juice
225g chilled butter, for layering

Place flour, first measure of butter, salt and Gingerbread Spice Mixture into a large mixing bowl and, using your fingers, roughly break up the butter into the flour. Add ice-cold water and lemon juice. Using your hands, mix ingredients to form a firm dough. Tip dough out onto a lightly floured surface and knead for 2–3 minutes. Form into a ball. Cover dough with clingfilm and allow to rest for 5–10 minutes. On a lightly floured surface, use a rolling pin to roll out dough to a 25cm square approximately 1cm thick.

Ensure layering butter is the same consistency as the dough – this can be done by hitting the chilled butter with a rolling pin to achieve a 17cm square (the hitting will be enough to soften the butter). Place it inside the rolled out square of dough.

Fold each corner of dough into the centre to encase layering butter in an envelope, obtaining two layers of dough and one layer of butter.

Now give pastry six 'single turns' as described in the Butter Puff Pastry recipe (see page 203) and cover with clingfilm. Store in refrigerator or freezer until needed.

Apricot Glaze

100g apricot jam
4 tbsp water

Place jam and water in a saucepan and bring
to the boil. Strain through a sieve and brush
on tart while both glaze and tart are hot.

Egg Wash

1 egg
2 tbsp water or milk

Mix together egg and water or milk until it's
very liquid and there are no globules of egg
white. If you want a really high shine, add an
extra egg yolk in.

Water Icing

140g icing sugar
¼ tsp softened butter
1 tbsp hot water (approximately)

In a small bowl, whisk together icing sugar,
butter and water until there are no more
lumps. You want the icing to drizzle off the
whisk nicely when you lift the whisk up out of
the bowl. Add a bit more icing sugar if it's too
wet or a little more water if it's too dry. Cover
and leave to sit for 5 minutes before using.

Cream Chantilly

200ml double cream
25g caster sugar
1 vanilla pod, split and seeds scraped out

Place cream, sugar and vanilla seeds into
a bowl and whisk until soft or stiff peaks
(depending on its use) form. Cover and place
in refrigerator until required. You may need to
re-whip it a little before serving to achieve the
required consistency.

Crème Pâtissière
(Pastry Cream)

250ml full-fat milk
4 egg yolks
50g granulated sugar
30g cornflour

In a saucepan, bring milk to the boil. In a
mixing bowl, beat egg yolks together with
sugar and cornflour. Pour hot milk over egg
mixture, beating all the time. Return mixture
to the saucepan and bring it back to a simmer,
stirring all the time. Remove from heat and
allow to cool.

Note: Crème Pâtissière should be made the
day before it is needed.

Gingerbread Spice Mixture

2 tbsp ground ginger
2 tbsp ground cinnamon
1 tbsp ground allspice
1 tbsp ground cloves
1 tbsp ground nutmeg

Shake all ingredients together in a jar with a lid. Store in the jar until needed.

Pork Pie Jelly

900g pork bones
2 pig's trotters
2 large carrots, chopped
1 onion, peeled and chopped
2 stalks celery, chopped
1 bouquet garni (bay leaf, thyme, parsley; tied together with string)
½ tbsp black peppercorns

Place pork jelly ingredients into a large saucepan and pour in enough water to just cover. Bring slowly to the boil, then reduce heat to a simmer. Cook for three hours over a low heat, skimming off any scum that rises to the surface, then strain stock through a fine sieve and discard the solids.

Pour strained stock into a clean pan and simmer over a medium heat until liquid has reduced to approximately 500ml.

Cranberry Filling

1 tsp powdered arrowroot
200ml cold water
150g dried cranberries
20g granulated sugar

In a small cup, stir arrowroot and 50ml of the cold water together to make a slurry. Place cranberries, the remaining water and sugar into a small saucepan and bring to the boil. Cook for 2–3 minutes over a low heat. Remove from heat and add arrowroot slurry, stir and return to the heat. Cook for 2 minutes to thicken, stirring occasionally. Place in a clean bowl, cover with clingfilm, cool and store in the refrigerator until needed the following day.

Spiced Apple Filling

1 tsp powdered arrowroot
100ml cold water
1 large Granny Smith apple, cored, peeled and diced into 1cm cubes
30g granulated sugar
1/8 tsp cinnamon

In a small cup, stir arrowroot and 50ml of the water together to make a slurry. Place apple, remaining water and sugar into a small saucepan and bring to the boil. Cook for 2–3 minutes over a low heat. Remove from heat and add arrowroot slurry, stir and return to heat. Cook for 2 minutes to thicken, stirring occasionally. Place in a clean bowl, cover with clingfilm, cool and store in the refrigerator until needed the following day.

Gingernut Biscuits

MAKES 16–18 BISCUITS

250g standard plain flour
2 tsp ground ginger
2 tsp bicarbonate of soda
¾ tsp ground cardamom
¾ tsp ground cinnamon
½ tsp ground coriander
¼ tsp freshly ground black pepper
¼ tsp salt
100g crystallised ginger, chopped
170g light soft brown sugar
125g butter
70g vegetable baking margarine
1 large egg
90g honey
100g Demerara sugar, for rolling the balls in

Sift flour, ground ginger, bicarbonate of soda, cardamom, cinnamon, coriander, pepper and salt into a medium bowl. Whisk to blend. Add crystallised ginger and set aside.

In a large bowl, beat brown sugar, butter and vegetable baking margarine with an electric mixer until creamy (do not over-beat; it will add too much air). Add egg and honey and beat until blended. Stir in flour mixture, mixing until just blended. Cover and refrigerate for 1 hour.

Preheat oven to 170°C (gas mark 3). Lightly spray two baking trays with non-stick cooking spray and cover with non-stick baking paper (the spray stops the paper from sliding).

Place Demerara sugar on a plate. Remove biscuit dough from refrigerator and divide into 16–18 equal-sized portions. Using wet hands, form dough into balls, then roll in sugar to coat completely. Place on prepared trays, spacing 5cm apart.

Bake in preheated oven until cracked on top but still soft to touch, 15–17 minutes. Cool on trays for 5 minutes before carefully transferring to cooling racks. Cool completely.

Caramelised Garlic Topping

2 heads garlic, separated into cloves
2 tbsp olive oil
2 tbsp water
1 tbsp balsamic vinegar
3 tbsp sugar
½ tsp salt
¼ tsp ground pepper
1 sprig fresh rosemary, chopped

In a saucepan of boiling water, blanch garlic for 5 minutes. Refresh in cold water. Peel, then set aside.

Place olive oil in a heavy frying pan over a medium heat. When simmering, add garlic and sauté for 2–3 minutes, taking care not to burn it. Add water and balsamic vinegar and as the mixture bubbles add sugar, salt, pepper and rosemary. Reduce heat to its lowest setting and simmer for 3–4 minutes until a syrup is formed and garlic is soft. Transfer to a bowl and cool until needed.

Techniques

Timing

Mise en place is a French term, meaning 'everything in its place'. When making pastry, whatever type, it's important to make it the day before, or in many cases well in advance and store it in the freezer. If doing the latter, take the pastry out and thaw it overnight in the refrigerator before rolling it. The pastry needs time to rest, recover and relax before using it.

Rolling Out

Sweet and Short Pastry

When rolling sweet pastry, always ensure the pastry is chilled and firm to the touch. It contains a high amount of butter and therefore can soften very quickly in a warm room. Roll sweet or short pastry in the coolest temperature possible.

Make sure you have a light dusting (not a snow storm) of flour on the bench underneath the pastry at all times. Always ensure you can move the pastry in a circular motion around the bench, just using enough flour to prevent it sticking.

Puff Pastry

The same principle applies when rolling puff pastry with regards to the flour on the bench and being able to continually move the pastry around in a circular motion. The major difference with puff pastry is that because of the way the fat is incorporated into the dough, it is a lot tougher and will tend to be very elastic when rolling out. So to prevent your baked products from shrinking during baking, take your time rolling the pastry. Always relax the pastry during rolling: when the pastry feels as though it is springing back all the time, simply lift the pastry up and allow it to shrink back in and relax for a few minutes before continuing rolling again. For best results when making pastry products that you have rolled yourself, actually make up the product, finish it off ready for baking and place it covered loosely in the refrigerator for at least 2–3 hours or, even better, overnight. This will prevent your pastry shrinking and going out of shape during baking. Of course this doesn't apply to store-bought pre-rolled pastry.

Rolling sweet pastry.   *Rolling puff pastry.*   *Lining a pie dish with puff pastry.*

Lining a Pie Dish, Tart Tin or Flan Ring with Pastry

Lightly brush the inside of the pie dish with oil or melted butter to give the pastry something to stick to. When lining a pie dish, tart tin or flan ring the most important thing is to ensure you don't stretch your pastry when pushing it into the corners at the bottom of the dish. If you do, it will shrink during baking, causing the filling to boil out and run down between the dish and pastry and making it stick.

Place the pastry in the bottom, flick or fold the excess pastry into the centre, then use your fingers to gently push the pastry into the corners and then work it up the sides. Press the pastry against the side of the dish until it reaches the top, then fold over the excess. Trim it level with a sharp knife before filling or leave it hanging over, fill and then brush with water before placing on lid. Trim off the excess, sealing the top to the bottom pastry.

Lining a flan tin with sweet pastry.
Shows tucking/pushing in the corners.

Baking Blind

Baking an unfilled flan or tart case before filling it is called baking blind. This technique is used when you want to put an unbaked filling inside a baked pastry case or when you want to ensure you don't get an under-baked soggy pastry bottom.

Baking blind is done by lining the flan or tart tin with your desired pastry and then snugly fitting baking paper or aluminium foil into the corners and up the sides. Then fill the pastry case with baking beans or rice and bake until the pastry has set or turned pale brown in colour. The paper and beans are removed and often the inside of the pastry case is brushed lightly with egg wash before returning it to the oven for 5–10 minutes to set. This helps keep the pastry nice and crisp when the filling goes inside, almost like a waterproof coating. Once the pre-baked pastry case has cooled, either the filling is added and then returned to the oven to bake, or the case is filled with a prepared and cooked filling, such as a custard or cream, which is further decorated before being ready to serve.

Clockwise from above: Lining the pastry with baking paper; Filling with beans or rice; Removing the beans and paper; Glazing with egg wash; Adding the filling.

Pie with fork holes in it.   *Pie with venting funnel (a bird).*

Venting Lidded Pies

The nature of fillings is that they contain a lot of moisture, so when topping any pie it is essential to create a vent within the lid to allow the steam to escape during baking. This prevents the filling boiling out over the edge of the pie and down the sides. The best way to create a vent is to first brush with egg wash and top the pie with any seeds, cheese or similar topping. Then, using a sharp pointed knife, cut two or three slits in the pastry or puncture it a few times with a fork. If you cut the pastry vents before brushing with egg wash, there is every chance you will fill in the slits or holes, making the venting pointless. For large, family-size pies you can often purchase a special venting pipe or funnel, usually in the shape of a blackbird, which is placed in the centre of the filling before the pastry lid is placed on top.

Glazing

There is only really one reason for glazing a pie, tart or flan and this is eye appeal and presentation. Most savoury-based recipes call for a simple egg wash made up of beaten egg and a dash of water or milk (see page 209). This is always done before baking and the higher the concentration of egg the shinier the glaze. To achieve maximum shine, many professional bakers use only egg white with a dash of milk to loosen it a little. If you don't have an egg handy, you can always use full-fat milk, as the milk sugar (lactose) will caramelise during baking, giving a small shine.

When glazing sweet fruit-based pies in which the fruit is exposed, it's common practice to apply an apricot glaze after the baking has been completed. This is always applied hot and when it sets it creates a wonderful, golden shine on the surface.

Egg wash before baking.   *Apricot glaze after baking.*

There is a second reason to use apricot glaze and that is to prevent the fruit from drying out. Once the apricot glaze has set, it will create a protective layer, preventing moisture loss.

You can also glaze the top of pastry with icing sugar, which should be done within the last 5 minutes of baking. Take the pie out of the oven, then very gently and lightly dust the top of the pastry and place it back into the oven to melt and caramelise the sugar, creating an extremely high gloss. Of course, this is only used on pies with a sweet filling inside.

Decorating

You can create a very eye-catching pie by simply decorating it before or after baking. It is all about finishing off and creating that little bit of extra eye appeal. Many commercial bakeries make their pies the same shape and add seeds, cheese, coarse breadcrumbs or even little strips of pastry to the tops before baking to signify the different fillings used in each pie. You can see from the many photos opposite that the sky is the limit with what you can do, so let your imagination go wild before and after baking. Just remember, keep the decorating simple so that it enhances and complements the filling.

FACING PAGE
1, 2: Scoring the pastry with the back of a knife;
3: Dusting with icing sugar; 4, 5, 6, 7: Decorating with pastry – trellis tops, shapes, cut-outs; 8, 9: Decorating with nuts around the edges and grated cheese on top.

Acknowledgements

As with all books there are so many people to thank, but top of my list is Aaron McLean, my trusted photographer and friend. He is a pleasure to work with and knows exactly how I think and reproduces it on film for all to enjoy. Check him out: www.aaronmclean.com

Thank you to Kate Stockman and Catherine O'Loughlin at Penguin Group (NZ) for allowing me to write and photograph the book with total confidence. It's always great to work with a talented team of professionals.

A big thank you to Gretchen Lowe, who took up the challenge to help me with this book and spent many, many hours in her kitchen, testing and writing countless recipes for this book. Gretchen's taste buds are one of her strong points and when I asked her to come up with some yummy combinations for pie fillings, she immediately sprung into action. Together we fine-tuned the pies into reality. I love working with people who love to learn, and throughout the photography Gretchen was great – and there with her apron on! Gretchen, I hope your 'food dreams' come true.

As always, Air New Zealand, Mike Tod and his team are great supporters and partners to everything I do globally and they flew me the many miles it took for me to complete this wonderful book for you to enjoy.

This book would not have been possible without the generous support of Jason Witehira of New World Victoria Park Supermarket, who supplied us with the mountain of ingredients needed. Jason is a true food advocate.

Thanks to Duncan Loney and his team at NZ Bakels for being true Pie Champions by creating and supporting the Bakels NZ Supreme Pie Awards, which has grown to be one of New Zealand's most recognised yearly food events, and for supporting all things pie related in this book.

To the team at Lantmännen Unibake UK, who have shared my love for creativity in bakery and certainly know great food when they see it. It's truly a great relationship and a wonderful place to work.

Also thanks to the young and talented Vivine Clarke for lending a hand in the book's photography and also for flying to Singapore to help out at my artisan bakery and foodstore Baker & Cook.

To Food TV New Zealand, who are great champions of my brand and baking. Thanks in particular to Julie Christie, Greg Heathcote and the exceptional team who work behind the scenes on the shows I am involved with.

To Arno Sturny, Renny Aprea and the AUT School of Patisserie and Baking, who once again came to my rescue by providing us with a great location and support for the enormous photography sessions. You are the unsung heroes of the baking world!

Paul Hansen . . . well, what can I say? Thank you, not only for the wonderful research and words for the History of the Humble Pie, but also for capturing the extract of pie-making when I was only a twinkle in my mum's and dad's eyes. You are a great friend – thank you so much for all your support over my entire career to date.

Happy baking and thank you!
Global Baker Dean Brettschneider

Index